NEW DART/

D1485297

by the Rev. H. HU(
(RECTOR OF MESHAW).

"The Forest of Dartmoor"

PART 1 - - **SOUTH-EAST.**

with Special Articles on "Some Ancient Records of Dartmoor Parishes," and on "Some Dartmoor Worthies," and each part will also contain a Poet's Corner. Part I. records a hitherto unknown poem of Robert Herrick's on the "Parish Soldier." p. 52, and a simple confession of his faith, p. 78.

Beautifully Illustrated.   Price 1/-   Postage 2d.
PART 2 — NOW READY.

The Forest of Dartmoor.

PART 2—SOUTH-WEST.

By the Rev. H. HUGH BRETON,

M.A.

(Rector of Meshaw, S. Molton).

PRINTED & PUBLISHED BY
HOYTEN & COLE,
39. WHIMPLE STREET, PLYMOUTH.
1932.

BEDFORD HOTEL

TAVISTOCK.

THE BEDFORD HOTEL, an imposing castellated Gothic building in the centre of the town, was erected about 1720 by Wriothesley, the third Duke of Bedford, for an occasional residence. It occupies a portion of the site of the Ancient Abbey, part of the refectory of which still remains, and which the Proprietor is pleased for his visitors to see. The Hotel is now replete with all modern requirements, for the comfort and convenience of visitors ; including Hot and Cold water in every bedroom. Central heating. Officially appointed by the Royal Automobile Club and the Automobile Association.

A charming adjunct is the delightful **Old Garden covering two acres.**

The extensive hotel yard is provided with excellent Garage accommodation. Posting in all its branches is done from here, and cars are let on hire.

Tavistock is by its geographical situation incomparably the most convenient centre in Devon and Cornwall for motoring and touring generally. Motorists making it their headquarters can visit any part of the two counties and return within the day, thereby avoiding the discomfort and waste of time in the packing which is involved in a continual change of habitation.

Salmon and Trout fishing, Golf (18 holes), Tennis, Croquet, Bowls, Hunting and Badminton in the winter.

UNDER PERSONAL SUPERVISION.

W. I. LAKE Proprietor.

TO

HIS ROYAL HIGHNESS,

EDWARD, PRINCE OF WALES,

AND

DUKE OF CORNWALL,

THIS DESCRIPTION OF HIS FOREST OF DARTMOOR,
DEVON.

Is humbly dedicated by the gracious permission of

𝔥𝔦𝔰 𝔚𝔬𝔶𝔞𝔩 𝔥𝔦𝔤𝔥𝔫𝔢𝔰𝔰 𝔓𝔯𝔦𝔫𝔠𝔢 𝔈𝔡𝔴𝔞𝔯𝔡,

MASTER FORESTER,

AND LORD WARDEN OF THE STANNARIES,

BY HIS LOYAL, FAITHFUL, AND MOST OBEDIENT SERVANT

H. HUGH BRETON.

Meshaw Rectory, Devon,
July 1st, 1931.

PREFACE.

I offer this little book to the public, the second part of a series of four on " The Forest of Dartmoor," hoping it will enable visitors and others to know more of this delightful playground.

All the profits will be devoted to Church Work.

I thank these friends warmly : —

Mr. Charles Brittan, the Dartmoor artist, for the drawing for the Cover.

Mr. H. W. Harding for his pen and ink sketches.

Mr. Hansford Worth for his photos.

Messrs. Martins, Ltd., for the Rajah photos.

To the Western Morning News for allowing me to publish their photo of Mr. Pengelley's Funeral.

Mr. H. J. Crook for his excellent photo of Shavercombe Falls.

Mr. C. C. Calmady for notes on the First Rajah and for the photo of Harry Terrell.

H. HUGH BRETON.

Meshaw Rectory,
    South Molton,
        June 1st, 1932.

Photo by]   SHAVERCOMBE FALLS.   [*Mr. H. J. Crook.*

ffOrest of Dartmoor

PART 2.

CHAPTER I.

THE UPPER VALLEYS OF THE ERME AND YEALM

I. 1. **Motor to Harford Church,** there leave your car at the schoolhouse on the south side of the Church, take lane R. which leads to Harford Gate which opens on the moor. Here take the path which leads north.

Just before reaching **Lower Piles** is a **Kistvaen** just before the stream, a feeder of the Erme, is reached. It has no Capstone but it is a good monument. It is 150 yards S. S.E. angle of Lower Piles enclosure. Measurements— 3 ft 7 in. long, 1 ft. 4 in. wide S. end, 2 ft. North end, depth 3 ft., 100 ft. S.E. stands a large stone, 110 ft. away from the Kistvaen is a small cairn 20 ft. diameter, the Kistvaen formerly covered by the cairn is now gone. The containing circle has seven stones still standing, diameter 15 ft.

2. **Higher Piles Wood** is a good specimen of an ancient Dartmoor Wood. (See Part I., p.p. 37, 39).

3. Keeping to the East side of the Erme in three miles **Brown Heath** is reached, here is an interesting group of remains.

A Kistvaen stood at the head of the stone row, but now it is muddled in the stones of the Cairn.

The Stone Row is double, and the circle at its north end; the row does not point to the centre of the circle, and the Cairn does not occupy the true centre of the circle, 90 ft. south of the curve the row touches another circle which lies on its east side. 450 ft. further south, the row touches and is partly lost in the wall of a pound which is on its west side. The pound encloses hut circles and it is unusual to find a pound wall interfering with a stone circle, and thus indirectly with an interment, since the row terminated in a Cairn formerly covering a Kistvaen.

Leaving Brown Heath regain the china clay railway line and follow it up to its termination. Here we are close to Huntingdon remains. (See Part I., p. 23).

I. 4. **Red Lake Clay Works** cover a lot of ground and have been worked considerably. Huge heaps of clay spoil the moor. At the house of the head man one seems to be on the roof of the world – so high. From here is swamp in every direction, so be careful how you pick your way. A train still leaves Bittaford once a day and returns in the evening, but like everything just now clay is hit rather hard.

I. 5. Now back to Harford Bridge. Here on the west side is a path which leads up to **Tristis Rock**. Follow this up to Tristis Rock, on the south side of which is a fine group of remains.

Yadsworthy Stone Row runs N. and S., terminating in south end in a circle which has been the retaining circle of a barrow; this is S.W. of Tristis Rock, and between it and the Rock is the retaining circle of another barrow enclosing a ruined Kistvaen, the latter circle is very perfect and consists of 12 stones, diameter 16 ft., and is very regular. Of the Kistvaen only south side remains ; there is no trace of the other stones or capstones.

I. 6. **Bullaven**. Standing at Tristis Rock on the opposite side of the valley is Bullaven Farm Hotel, here one may stay and thoroughly enjoy the surrounding moor. The equipment is very up-to-date, and the charges reasonable.

I. 7. From Tristis Rock continue two miles north, gaining the high ground. The Tumulus is **Hillson's Hut** named after a man named Hillson, who made his home there for years. The Cairn is surrounded by **an earth Circle** instead of stone.

I. 8. Half-a mile W. of Hillsons Hut is **Stall Moor Row** a very fine stone row with large stones, it can be seen a great distance away.

I. 9. **Beehive Hut** on the Erme. If from the stone row you go on in a N. direction, in less than one mile you come down into a small lateral valley of the Erme, quite near the Erme in this little valley is a beehive hut, which was no doubt used by the Tinners in Elizabethan times.

I. 10 **Erme Valley Stone Row**. A mile north from the beehive hut is **a circle**, 42 ft diameter, with stones. From the circle starts the longest stone row in the British Isles. It runs uphill and down dale for $2\frac{1}{3}$ miles and terminates in the Cairn on the top of Green Hill; most of the stones as it ascends Green Hill are lost, either sunk in the bossy soil or taken away. The Row crosses the Erme half-mile below Red Lake and then begins its ascent of Green Hill.

I. 11. **Erme Head**. From Red Lake the Erme may easily be followed up to Erme Head where are many tinner's heaps, the remains of considerable workings about here.

CHAPTER II.

CORNWOOD.

II. 1. **Hawns and Dendles**. is a great resort of Plymouthians for a day's outing or an afternoon ramble, and is reached by going to Coombe, from there take the footpath up the valley which runs just above the Yealm (part I., IX., 4); or to North Hele Farm and keep straight on until the road is reached at Dendles Green. From this point after crossing the river, Broadall Lake may be ascended.

In about half mile an old wall will be reached, cross it, and in 200 yards cross a second wall; here you will be out on the open moor; from here it is easy to follow the Broadall Lake up the Broadall Gulf to the stream's source under Pen Beacon. Just before a third wall is reached, are the remains of a prehistoric settlement with its Pounds and Hut Circles (part I., IX., 7). At Broadall Hut is swampy ground.

II. 2. Dendles Waste Circle. (See part I., IX., 7).

II. 3. **Stall Moor Stone Row** is 1,200 ft. long. (See I., 8). From Cornwood go to Wisdom Mill, then on past Tor, keep right away from the river, about one mile you come to the open moor, here ascend the hill to the Row. Not

STONE ROW ON STALL MOOR.

far from the north end is a small stone circle in the Row. This Row should be seen by all Dartmoor visitors.

II. 4. **Pen Beacon** is reached from Cornwood by going to West Rook Farm and from there follow the lane to West Rook Gate which opens on to the moor; from here ascend.

Pen Beacon Stone Row is less than 150 yards south of the Beacon, and consists of 8 stones; length 66 ft., and is 20 yards west of the old reave wall which runs south from the Beacon.

Pen Tumulus crowns the hill which is 1,404 ft. above sea level.

Pen Tumulus and Stone Row. About $\frac{1}{3}$ mile west of the Stone Row this will be found. It consists of a Tumulus and a few stones of a Stone Row running S.W. from the Tumulus. $\frac{1}{3}$ mile S.E. of this monument is a **Third Tumulus** which has a containing circle of 12 stones, 20 ft. in diameter.

II. 5. **Shell Top** is $\frac{3}{4}$ mile N. of Pen Beacon and is reached by a footpath trodden by cattle. Shell Tor is a very prominent cluster of rocks, really a small tor, in the south west portion of Dartmoor.

II. 6. **Yealm Valley.** The Yealm is a beautiful river, and although so short it is well worth a visit. It tumbles out of the bogs from which the Shavercombe Brook also takes its rise, coming from a great height (1,500 ft.), it proceeds in a series of cascades and enters Dendles Wood and so on. On the left bank is a ruined Blowing House, and lying about are two mould stones, one of which is within the ruins.

By following the river upward and crossing it near Yealm Rocks a clitter of granite blocks – the ruins of another Blowing House will be found, within the ruins is a mould stone

It we follow the river down we pass through Dendles Wood and back to Cornwood.

CHAPTER III.

LEE MOOR.

III. 1. **Lee Moor** though spoilt by the clay works has some very interesting remains close at hand on W. side of Crownhill Down, 1 mile South of the Lee Moor Clay Works, close to the huge clay dump. 100 yds. north of this Tumulus is a stone circle, diameter 16 ft., and seven stones remain. 150 yards S.S.W. of the Tumulus is a group of six barrows, five of which are arranged in a semi-circle.

III. 2. On the east side of Collard Tor and quite near the rocky summit are **Collard Stone Rows,** about 120 ft. and 100 ft. in length respectively. One leads to a dilapidated circle, the other led up to a cairn which has been removed. Just below them now is the row of Collard Tor Cottages, which will help you find them.

III. 5. **Chambered Hut,** now in ruins, was a hut cluster with several chambers. To reach it, back to the main road near Lee Moor House, and on to the end of the wall of the enclosures attached to the cottages on the right; here take the path east which will lead you comfortably across the rough ground and the leats. At $\frac{5}{8}$ of a mile from the road the path ends, and at about 300 yards east of this point you will find the Chambered Hut in a very dilapidated condition, but at one time it was a cluster of human dwellings.

III. 6. Next back to the road to the point from which you started, **Lee Moor House** is on the right in its own grounds and is the property of Mr. Martin, who now lives at Slade, Cornwood. The rhododendrons in these groups in May and June are splendid.

III. 7. Just beyond Lee Moor House on right side of the road is **Blackaton Cross,** also called Romans Cross. The head of the cross and its base formed part of an ancient cross, but the shaft had been destroyed. The present shaft was a stone made for a window sill at Lee Moor House and was given by the late Mr. Phillips, who many years ago lived there. This public spirited man set the cross up again in its ancient base, adding the window sill for a shaft.

III. 7. **Emmets Post** is an upright stone fixed in a Tumulus. The stone is the bond stone between the lands of Sir Henry Lopes, Bart., and the Earl of Morley. From the post the path may be followed west to Shaugh Prior. This is a path used much by the workmen at the clay works as they go to and fro their work.

III. 8. The road we have just left leads on to Cadover Bridge. Follow the road on to a point where there is a short steep hill. On the moor on left is a **large pound,** containing several hut circles, the stones of the pound wall can be seen from the road.

CHAPTER IV.

CADOVER BRIDGE.

From this delightful spot many are the interests of the wayfarer. This story was told me which happened about this spot. During the Great Frost of 1855, there was a very heavy fall of snow. A Rev. Patey, Master of the Grammar School at Plympton, used to ride over to

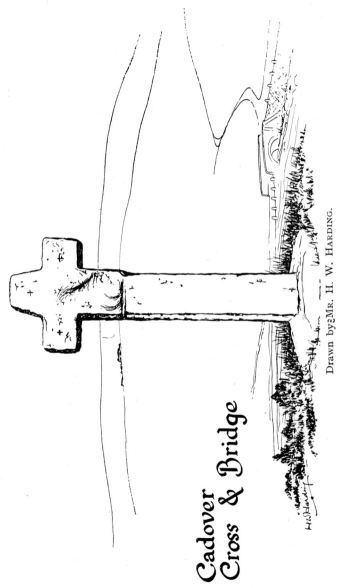

Cadover Cross & Bridge

Drawn by Mr. H. W. HARDING.

Sheepstor from Plympton, on Sundays, to take the service. One Sunday after this fall of snow he was on the moor all day, and never reached Sheepstor, but had to return home. At times he had to get off and tread the snow to make it hard enough for the pony to walk on. He was unable to go for two or three Sundays, and when he arrived at Sheepstor again, he was told that he was the first outsider they had seen in the parish for three weeks. Exactly the same thing was told to a man who came into Sheepstor three weeks after the blizzard of 1891.

IV. 1. **To Shaugh Prior** take road to right and then turn right again at the first turning.

IV. 2. **Cadover Cross** was re-erected by me in 1915. It lay on the ground for many years near where it stands now. I gave it a new shaft and set it up.

IV. 3. In 1873 this cross was noticed lying down by the soldiers encamped on Ringmoor Down, and they set it up on the soil, but it had fallen again. When I had fixed a new shaft to the fine head, we were wondering where to fix it, and chose a green sward in the heather. We were digging a hole for the shaft intending to set it in cement, when we came across a large block of stone. This proved to be the original socket stone *in situ*. It had this unusual feature, the socket hole was 13 inches deep and *quite perforated the stone*. So all we had to do was to fix it in its original position—a very satisfactory restoration.

Note this cross has three small incised crosses on its face, one on the head, and one on each of the arms—no other Dartmoor Cross is like this.

IV. 4. This is the country of Dewer, the wild huntsman, who with his fire-breathing hounds hunts the moor on dark stormy nights.

> " All night long in the dark and the Wet,
> Dewer goes riding by."

IV. 5. **Cadworthy Kistvaen**. Follow the wall near the cross and pass Cadworthy Farm which is below, on the south side of the wall. Keep to the wall until it suddenly bends towards the river, at this bend is the Kistvaen which has its containing stone circle, but the stones are all prostrate.

DEWER, THE WILD HUNTSMAN

From this point go on to

IV. 6. **Carrington Rock,** which overlooks the valley of the Plym, and the view is very fine.

Note, as you approach the rock the hill has been forti-fied, and has a stone wall round it except west and south.

The Dewerstone, a fine crag, is just below.

IV. 7. **Wigford Circle** is on the top of Wigford Down. It has only four stones, which are huge slabs ; the cairn which they enclosed was carted away some years ago ; 26 cart loads were taken away. Also near by are the ruins of two large cairns.

IV. 8. From the pond follow the road west towards Hooe Meavy. At $\frac{1}{2}$ mile take to the moor along a grassy track on left side of the road. In 200 yards are the remains of a small circle, which is 40 yards in a straight line from the road. The diameter is 30 ft., but only a semi-circle is left. Only six stones remain, the largest of which is four ft. 300 yards further south west is the junction of four green paths, here is a stone circle almost complete. There are 18 stones, diameter 30 ft. This circle has been the containing circle of a large cairn, which has long ago been carted away.

Both these circles are on a raised platform, and the stones, most of them are of the slab type, laid long ways.

They have been much alike and about the same size.

IV. 9. **Good a-Meavy Cross.** Along the road referred to about $\frac{1}{2}$ mile on, you come to a place where four ways meet. Here turn left, and on to Good-a-Meavy. On the moor just outside the gate we enter to turn down to Good-a-Meavy, stands Good-a-Meavy Cross. On its site originally stood the base of an ancient cross which pointed the way to the ford below. This was taken away some years ago, and is now in the grounds of Good-a-Meavy House, and forms the base there of a memorial cross to Mr. Hill's son, who was killed at the Dardanelles during the war. Mr. Hill very generously consented to place the present cross on the green where it is, and I was present when it was completed.

IV. 10. Below Good-a-Meavy House the Meavy flows on its way to meet the Plym at Shaugh Bridge. It is very pretty about here; after crossing the bridge the road leads on to Roborough Down.

IV. 11. Back to the Four Ways and go on down to Hooe Meavy. This was a lovely glen before the trees were cut down during the war. Cross Hooe Meavy Bridge and pass through **Clearbrook.**

At Clearbrook the road runs south west across Roborough Down and meets the main road (Plymouth to Yelverton). As you come out on to the main road on the right hand side an ancient cross-base stood, but a few years ago it disappeared; it was fractured but that it was a cross-base is beyond dispute. No doubt it marked the way leading to Hooe Meavy and the moor beyond.

About half-way along the road between Brisworthy Pond and Hooe Meavy is a cross-base beside the road.

CHAPTER V.

SHAUGH.

From the halt bearing this name some delightful rambles may be made.

V. 1. **Shaugh Bridge,** one mile, is situated at the entrance of the gorge of the Plym, and is a favourite resort of picnic parties

The scenery here is very grand, and a walk should be taken up the gorge as far as the Dewerstone.

Old Shaugh Bridge was destroyed by a great flood on January 27th, 1823, which was caused by the sudden melting of a deep snow accompanied by a deluge of rain, a combination which causes nearly all very exceptional floods on Dartmoor.

V. 2 **Plym Gorge,** which is entered at Shaugh Bridge, is one of the most picturesque on the moor. It is seen to best advantage either from the top of the Dewerstone or from the path above the Clay works which winds up the south side of the Gorge to Cadover Bridge. On its northern side are five distinct spurs of rock which rise out of the woods which clothe the sides of the Gorge. The finest of these is :—

V. 3. The Dewerstone, a magnificent precipice, whose base is lapped by the limpid waters of the Plym, and whose beetling crags are still the home of the raven. A few hundred yards up stream the Plym plunges over a bar of granite forming a small but charming cascade.

V. 4. Carrington Rock. This is a stiff climb from Shaugh Bridge, but one which is attempted by nearly all visitors, except the infirm and the indolent. After crossing the wooden

ONE OF THE NEW BENCH-ENDS IN
SHEEPSTOR CHURCH.
THE VINE AND THE DOVE.

bridge, a zigzag path winds up to the Rock, from which there is a magnificent view. Carrington's name and the date are cut on the face of the highest rock. The return to the bridge may be made by descending the footpath on the south side of the Rock.

A walk from the Rock to Sheepstor is described in walk (24) of my Sheepstor chapter

There are the remains of an ancient camp on this hill, above the Dewerstone.

V. 5. **Shaugh Church** ($1\frac{1}{2}$ miles) is a fine old moorland shrine, with an imposing tower which is a landmark for miles.

The church was struck by lightning in 1823.

Shaugh has one of the finest font covers in the county. It is made of oak and beautifully carved. Just over 30 years ago it narrowly escaped destruction.

This splendid work of art was accounted as unfit to adorn the sanctuary of God, and it was cast out of the sanctuary as a worthless and unholy thing, and placed in a barn. Providentially it was rescued and restored to the church, and it again adorns and beautifies—

> ". . . . the sacred Font,
> And there the Holy Dove
> To pour is ever wont
> His blessings from above."

Note the stone quatre-partite groined roof in the porch.

There is a base of an octagonal cross in the church-yard on the south side of the church, and a good speci-men of the Dartmoor cross is built into the vicarage hedge, and will be seen on the right as one passes up the road. This road leads out on to Shaugh Moor.

Where the road enters on the moor, about 100 yards north, beside the road is another cross. There is another cross base near the cross roads where the Wattor road meets the Plympton road.

To Shaugh Moor which is covered with antiquities of one sort and another. See Collard Stones Rows (III. 2).

On Shaugh Beacon is a curious stone which has been used as a Cromlech at some time. It is really nature's work, but there is no doubt it has formed part of a cromlech.

Shaugh Barrow. From Shaugh Church take the road to
Cadover Bridge, on reaching the open moor turn left.
Soon as you approach Shaden Brake on right side of the
road you will see this fine barrow.

Shaugh Circle and Stone Row. From the barrow at a
distance of 360 ft. east will be found these remains.

The circle is at the south end of the row, and has still
three stones standing, and three down. It has a diameter
of 51 ft., the row points slightly east of the circle. The
stones of the row are small, but it is very perfect, except
that a few stones were taken away just before I found it in
1917.

Shaugh to Trowlesworthy Circle and Stone Rows. To
Cadover Bridge, then turn to the left, and take the first
turning to the left again to Trowlesworthy Warren.
Trowlesworthy is a very ancient tenement, and is referred
to in a deed dated 1290. After passing by the Warren
House, with its curious courtyard, strike the leat 100
yards above the house. In less than a mile, southwards,
the leat passes right through the antiquities. On its north
bank is the circle of eight stones, 23 ft. in diameter ; and a
very fine double stone row, 420 ft. long, which the leat cuts
in two. It runs down to the base of the hill, where it
terminates in a large menhir, which has been moved a few
yards away from its original position.

On the west side of the leat, opposite the circle, is
another fine stone row, 250 ft. long, terminating in a
blocking stone. It formerly led up to a circle which
needs restoring. Some of its stones are under the turf.
The hillside above the leat is strewn with antiquities. The
old tenant at Trowlesworthy, John Lavers, died on
March 15th, 192 , in the ninety-fifth year of his age.
The moor was covered with a deep snow on the day of
his funeral, but the March sun melted it 3 ft. in the day.

CHAPTER VI.

BRISWORTHY.

VI. 1.   At Brisworthy, outside the farm as you enter the lane to go down to Brisworthy Burrows, is a large boulder close to the gate.   Note it has 17 dents in it, this was an old mortar stone, and belonged to a Blowing House which formerly stood in the field on the other side of the stone wall, just inside the gate.

VI. 2.   When this lane comes out on the moor follow the wall westward.   In 100 yards in a corner is the site of a blowing house ; two mortar stones are there now, and some years ago Mr. R. Hansford Worth found an old furnace base stone, which alas ! has disappeared and can nowhere be found.

VI. 3.   **Brisworthy Circle.**   This is a very fine specimen of the stone circle, and is situated at the southern extremity of Ringmoor Down, where the ground slopes down to Legis Lake.

The Down probably takes its name from this ring of stones.

It is very easily found if one strikes the wall which runs from Brisworthy Plantation eastwards down to the Legis Lake.   This wall divides the moorland from the new-takes of Brisworthy Farm.

If visitors who are motoring or driving, desire to visit this interesting monument, they should drive to Brisworthy Farm and leave their conveyance there, and then take the lane which leads north-eastwards, which will soon bring them out on to the moor, and which passes close by the circle.   As they approach the moor the circle will be seen ahead.   The circle is one of the finest on Dartmoor, although the Grey Wethers and Scor Hill are larger specimens.   Its diameter is about 80 ft., and it consists of 24 stones.   All except three lay prostate on the ground until the summer of 1909, when Mr. R. Hansford Worth and I re-erected the stones of this fine monument.

Several stones are missing on the south side, which are evidently in the wall near by.

One stone on the west side, is a very curious shape, having a slight resemblance to the very curious stone in the pulpit circle near Trowlesworthy,

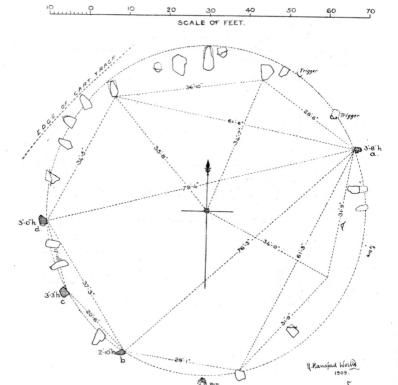

BRISWORTHY CIRCLE

SCALE OF FEET.

Excavations in the centre disclosed the presence of wood ashes and charcoal,

Mrs, Wheeler, at Brisworthy Farm, will provide tea for visitors,

VI. 4, **Brisworthy Tumulus** will be found 50 yards to the east of the circle, where the ground slopes down towards Legis Lake.

Little more than the site now remains, with two stones of the small enclosing circle.

Here again digging operations disclosed the presence of charcoal. There are traces of a stone row which formerly ran from the tumulus down to the lake.

LEGIS LAKE KISTVAEN.

VI. 5. **Legis Lake Kistvaen** is situated 300 yards N.N.E. of the circle.

This is a very fine and complete specimen of the kistvaen, although not nearly so large as those at Cadworthy or at Drizzlecombe. It is very complete, and evidently has an enclosing circle, the stones of which are all down.

A stone row originally led up to it from the westward, but only a few stones of it remain now.

C

This kistvaen seems to have been unknown to the present generation, until I discovered it in the spring of 1908. To find it, get the gate in the wall and the clay heap in a line.

VI. 6. Ringmoor Circle and Stone Row. These remains are not difficult to find, if the following directions are followed.

After leaving the kistvaen and proceeding a few yards to the N.W., the remains of a low reeve wall will be struck, which time and weather have nearly obliterated. The grassy reeve runs westward. If this be followed about 200 yards it will be found at the top of the hill to pass right through the stone row which leads up to the circle.

$\frac{1}{2}$ m. N. *almost* in a line with the end stone is Sheepstor circle. It is quite a small circle, 23 ft. diameter, and encloses a barrow. Note, the stones on south side are the largest. 200 yards east is another small barrow.

Ringmoor circle doubtless originally enclosed a cairn, and is 42 ft. in diameter, and now consists of ten stones, only three of which were standing.

The stone row, which is a single row for some distance and then double, runs N.E. for 450 yards, and many of the stones, especially at the further end, are buried under the heather.

Nearly all the stones of this monumenet were re-erected by the Rev. S. Baring-Gould, Mr. R. Hansford Worth, and myself in August, 1911.

VI. 7. Sites of Seven Tumuli will be found if the track from Sheepstor circle be followed across Ringmoor Down until you approach a stone wall. If before reaching the wall you turn and set your course due N., you will find on the slope of the hill the remains of seven tumuli which have formed huge cairns at some time. If the wall be followed up, remains of an eighth tumulus is found near the wall on its west side.

VI. 8. Gutter Tor Hut Circles. These very fine specimens of the hut circle will be found near the wall on its east side, and to the south side of the postman's walk.

Gutter Tor Kistvaen. The remains of a small kistvaen will be seen on the west side of the wall, and about 100 yards from the wall by the hut circle　Alas, only the enclosing stones remain.

Gutter Tor Rock Basin will be found on the top of the southern rock of the tor. It is a very fair specimen.

VI. 9. **Nattor Tumulus** is easily found, whether approaching from Sheepstor village or from Gutter Tor.

From Sheepstor the road which runs by Colyton out on to the moor, and which passes Nattor Farm, should be followed until you get to a thorn bush standing near a gate – on the opposite side of the road is the tumulus, which has been a very large one. It has no enclosing circle of stones.

CHAPTER VII.

DITSWORTHY WARREN.

VII. 1. **Sheepstor to Ditsworthy Warren** (three miles).

A very pleasant walk from Sheepstor. Follow the lane beyond Sheepstor Church past Colyton. Just above the farm you pass through a gateway on to the moor. Then *either* keep straight on to Burracombe Gate, and then take the track to the right, which will lead you to the Warren House, which is just below the low tor ahead.

At the gate above Colyton, which I have mentioned, take the footpath on the moor which runs parallel with the road for some distance and then passes directly over Gutter Tor. At the top of the tor the path will be seen below, winding its way to the Warren House.

Or still another way. At the gate above Colyton take the footpath across the top of Ringmoor to Ringmoor Gate. Here you join the road to the Warren, which should be followed.

3, 4, 17.　　　3, 16.　　　3, 15.

VII. 2. **To Drizzlecombe Antiquities** (four miles). At the back of the Warren House is a track which passes right by the remains on its way to Plym Steps. (The track which turns off to the left leads to Eylesbarrow).

Along the track you presently come to a ruined kistvaen. Here you can begin your explorations. A rough plan of the remains is given on my plan of antiquities.

They consist of three stone rows leading to cairns, enclosed in stone circles. Each row ends in a menhir, which forms the blocking stone. View the Great Menhir, which is 18 ft. high from all sides. On the north side it has a most weird

DRIZZLECOMBE MENHIR AND ROW.

appearance. In this wild and desolate country this great menhir has for thousands of years kept its lonely watch over its honoured dead. The foot of man seldom passes by, but—

> " At noon the wild bee hummeth
> About the mossed headstone ;
> At midnight the moon cometh,
> And looketh down alone."

Near by is the Giant's Grave, the largest cairn on the moor. 290 yards north of the cairn is the large kistvaen on a low mound. At the north west foot of the cairn is a tiny kistvaen.

The whole of this desolate country is strewn with the monuments of the dead, for this was the great cemetery of the town which covered a good portion of the hill to the north west, in the direction of Burracombe Gate.

In retracing our steps towards Sheepstor, if we examine this hill we shall find the ruins of huts in all directions.

DITSWORTHY WARREN.

Many of the huts seem to have been so deep, a feature which suggests that the prehistoric men who lived here possessed the luxury of capacious wine cellars.

The easiest way back to Sheepstor is to proceed N.N.W. from Drizzlecombe and to strike the rough road from Eylesbarrow.

3, 16, 19.   4, 3.

VII. 3. **To Plym Steps** (six miles). Route same as VII. 2 as far as the Giant's Grave. From this point follow

Photo by]   DRIZZLECOMBE MENHIR.   [*Mr. R. C. Letheren.*

the path right up the Plym Valley. The stream which
meets the Plym where the river bends is the Langcombe.
Just above are Plym Steps. On the bank of the river is
an old blowing house.

Just before reaching the Langcombe, you see on your
left hand a fine pound and a cairn on its S.W. side.

Follow the Plym up till you come to the Abbot's Ford.

DITSWORTHY WARREN KITCHEN.

The most direct way to Plym Steps is to take the track
from Burracombe Gate to Eylesbarrow Mine Ruin, $\frac{1}{2}$ mile
before reaching the ruin take the cart track which turns
right. The cart track ascends the rising ground beyond
the stream and leads across the moor to Plym Steps and
the Langcombe Valley. The tors passed on the left are
Higher and Lower Harter Tors.

VII. 4. **To Deadman's Bottom and Grim's Grave at
Langcombe Head** (six miles.) Route same as VII. 3 to the
point where the Langcombe joins the Plym. Here cross

the Plym and ascend the hill. On the top of the hill, a
little to the left, will be found Plym Steps Kistvaen, surrounded by a nice circle of stones, which are all down.
The tor to the north is Calveslake Tor. On its eastern
slopes is another kistvaen.

Continuing one's walk eastward, you soon come to
Deadman's Bottom. Here, well above the river, on your
left will be found an interesting group of remains—two
fine kistvaens in ruins and two circles which were used as
crematoria.

In the little rill, which comes from the marshy ground
above in Deadman's Bottom, are most exquisite mosses
of all shades and colours, the prettiest I have ever seen.

Continuing one's walk to the head of the Langcombe,
Grim's Grave lies close to the stream. It is a very fine
kistvaen, second only to Lakehead Kistvaen near Post-
bridge; but the kistvaen at Deadman's Bottom will be still
finer if carefully restored, as the capstone is so very large.

In dry weather, by striking N.E. from Grim's Grave,
you can reach Broad Rock, but it is marshy ground, as it
is near the head of the Erme.

VII. 5. **To Shavercombe and Hen Tor** (four miles).
Start at Ditsworthy Bridge, which is just below the Warren
House. After crossing the bridge, take the track to the
left, which will bring you to Shavercombe, which is the
next dip in the hills. Here is a sweet little dell, such as
one would least expect to find in such a desolate part of
the moor.

In the little gorge is a waterfall, which is very fine after
rain (See Frontispiece). 150 yards S.S.W. of the waterfall
is a fine kistvaen, and nearly 300 yards S.E. of this monument are the ruins of another.

Here strike across the moor for Hen Tor, which is a fine
pile of rocks. Ascend the tor from its east side, which is
quite easy.

On the top of the tor, facing west, is a recess, where
one can lie full length and bask in the sun, quite sheltered
from a cold east wind.

On descending from the tor, you can make your way

back to Ditsworthy Bridge through the ruins of Hen Tor
Farm, which has been tenantless for more than a hundred
years.

The old saying, "Drive the natural away and it returns
at a gallop," is well illustrated on the slopes of Hen Tor,
where formerly there was Hen Tor Farm, which was
abandoned a century ago.   Nature has so rapidly resumed
her sway that most of the traces of the farm have disappeared.

VII. 6.   **To Ditsworthy Circle, Willing's Wall Circle and
Kistvaen** (4 miles).   After crossing Ditsworthy Bridge,
bear to the right.   You soon come to the Hen Tor Brook.
Just before you reach it you will come upon a very interesting hut circle.   It has a protecting wall on its S.W.
side, built to protect its prehistoric tenants from the bad
weather.

Next proceed S.E. towards Willing's Wall.   About 200
yards on the north side of the wall, and not far from the
east bank of Hen Tor Brook, you will find Ditsworthy
Circle, which formerly enclosed two kistvaens, the cover
stones of which are still among the ruins.   The circle
consists of 16 stones and is about 23 ft. in diameter, and
is very dilapidated, and much hidden by the heather.

Next strike Willing's Wall, and then follow it in the
westerly direction.   It soon crosses the Hen Tor Brook.
About 100 yards from the brook, near the north side of
the wall, is a good specimen of the kistvaen.

Continuing one's walk to the top of the hill, about half
way between Hen Tor Brook and Spanish Lake, Willing's
Wall Circle will be found.   It consists of six clusters of
three or four stones in each cluster, erected at intervals.
Some of the stones are down.   The diameter of the circle
is about 140 ft.   The wall has been built into the southern
arc of the circle, and has taken some of its stones.

VII. 7.   **To Spanish Lake, Shell Top, Pen Beacon and
Cornwood.**   Cross the Plym by the stones where it is
joined by Spanish Lake.   Ascend the little dell formed
by Spanish Lake ; near the head of the dell turn left up
the hill.   As there is a considerable swamp at the head of

Spanish Lake, which also covers a good deal of ground towards Shell Top, it will be necessary to keep up well on the high ground. When Shell Top, which is a small tor, comes into view, get to the head of the swamp and then strike out for Shell Top; thence is only a short mile on to Pen Beacon, from which a low reeve wall runs to Shell Top. Along its east side runs a little path—a sheep track. If this be followed, Pen Beacon is easily ascended. On the west side of the beacon, a few yards away, is a fine hut circle. From the beacon descend into Cornwood across the slopes of Cornwood Common. (See II. 4).

From Shell Top, Hen Tor is only 1 mile about due north. The ground between the two tors is rather rough.

From Spanish Lake, Great and Little Trowlesworthy Tors are easily ascended. There is a ruined wall on the north slope of Great Trowlesworthy Tor called "Irishmen's Wall."

CHAPTER VIII.

SHEEPSTOR.

THE COUNTRY DANCES.   VENVILLE RIGHTS.

1—*The Village Cross.*   2—*The Lych Gate.*   3—*The Church
and the Churchyard Cross.*   4—*The Well of St. Leonard.*
5—*The Bull Ring.*   6—*The Rajah's Tomb.*

SHEEPSTOR VILLAGE.

NOWHERE on Dartmoor is there a place so beautiful and
fair as the quaint and picturesque little village of Sheepstor. Nestling under the great tor from which it takes its
name, it is well sheltered from the mountain winds.

From the brow of Yennadon—

" Deep lies the valley, girt with rock and wood,
    In rural wise the scattered hamlet stood,—
    Lake, crag, cascade adorn the scene,
    Gardens and fields and shepherds' walks between,
    Through all, a streamlet, from its mountain source
    Seen but by stealth, pursues its rocky course."

This old-world hamlet was famed in years gone by for its exceedingly pretty country dances and its clever old fiddler, William Andrew, who knew all the dance tunes.

THE SUNDIAL, SHEEPSTOR.

The dear old fiddler has gone to his rest years ago, but the old country dances are still preserved, and may be seen at the Harvest Festivals.

" Sheepstor is the most truly rural parish in Devonshire." These were the words used a few days ago by a diocesan official who knows every corner of Devonshire to convey to me the impression Sheepstor always gives him.

Sheepstor is one of the few parishes still in Venville. In return for a fine we pay to the Duchy, we have certain rights. On the Duchy lands we can pasture ponies and cattle, cut peat for our fires, and take away anything from the moor which may do us good, except green oak and venison. As the oak tree does not grow on the Duchy lands in this neighbourhood, and the deer is extinct on Dartmoor, there is no fear of our rights being exceeded.

The Venville rights originated many hundreds of years ago. Several of the explanations of their origin which I have seen are incorrect. They were originally granted to the farmers in return for the services they rendered to the Forester in assisting him in exterminating the wolves which infested the forest long after they were extinct in other parts of England. As evidence that wolves infested English forests later than is generally supposed, there is an interesting tomb of a Bishop of Wells in Wells Cathedral, dated about 1200, on which are recorded the noble deeds of the prelate. One of his exploits recorded was the material assistance which he rendered in exterminating the wolves in the great forest of Mendip by hunting.

VIII. 1. **The Village Cross.** As we enter the old church town, with its truly rural surroundings, the first object that arrests our attention is the ancient cross, standing on a rugged but very substantial base. In 1910, the cross was restored to its rightful place in the middle of the parish. For a great number of years it has been used as a rubbing-post for cattle, and previous to that as a gate-post. We recently gave it new arms, and the men of Sheepstor combined and built the large base and re-erected the cross as a memorial of the Coronation of H.M. King George V. The men nobly devoted their evenings to the work for three weeks without any remuneration.

This is the fine old spirit of self-sacrifice and self-devotion, which has been the means of building many of our fine country churches centuries ago.

We hope the old cross may stand on Sheepstor Green for many centuries to come, as a witness to their work and labour of love.

In shape there is no other on the moor quite like it, while the cross in relief on both sides is not found on any other Dartmoor cross.

The cross is seen very well outside the church porch, and whenever a coffin rests on the coffin stone of the lych gate, the cross, being in a line, stands immediately above it. This is a very impressive feature, and quite undesigned. It was dedicated by the vicar on the afternoon of Coronation Day—June 22nd, 1911—in order that it may be used as a preaching cross, and open-air services held there.

The Fine War Memorial Cross which stands opposite the Church door was erected in memory of William Mortimore and Harry Blatchford who gave their lives for their country.

VIII. 2. **The Lych Gate** is a very fine specimen. Its crumbling oak beams testify to its great age.

A small pedestal for a saint will be noticed on the wall of the house outside the lych gate.

VIII. 3. **The Church.** The church is a typical Dartmoor church in the perpendicular style. Its large square embattled tower has turrets at each corner with fine crocketted pinnacles.

The tower contains a peal of six bells, five of which were cast in 1769. One bears the inscription, " I call the quick to church and the dead to grave." Through the very praiseworthy efforts of my predecessor, the Rev. H. Leigh Murray, the five bells were re-hung and a sixth added in 1904, and now there is a beautiful peal.

The weather-beaten tower is of great beauty, and the turrets and pinnacles yellow with a beautiful lichen. Here

> " Alone, and warming his five wits,
>   The white owl in the belfry sits."

In the north wall is a monument to the sister-in-law of Sir Francis Drake, and another to the memory of one of the Elfords.

The organ was completely renovated in 1909 at a cost of over £100.

A fine octagonal cross, recently repaired, is fixed in the stile to the south of the church porch. The shaft has been there a great number of years. The cross stands

THE BULL RING.

seven feet above the level of the ground, and was formerly much taller. I found another piece of the shaft in the wall at the side of the stile, but it was broken. The broken piece is now in the corner of the base of the Village Cross.

There are the remains of a very curious sundial over the church porch, which bears the initials of John Elford, of Longstone, and is dated 1640. It also has the following inscriptions :—" Et hora sic vita "; " Mors janua vitae." It consists of a skull and cross-bones, resting on an hour-glass, with ears of corn sprouting from the eye sockets. It is symbolical of " life out of death."

The Rood Screen was completed at Easter, 1914, at a cost of £450, and was dedicated on May 13th by the Lord Bishop of Exeter. One door and other fragments of the original fifteenth century screen are incorporated in the new Screen. This magnificent Screen consists of nine bays with beautiful tracery, and is 28 ft. long. The vaulting is exquisitely done. The panels of the vaulting and also the cornice is adorned with very elaborate car-

CRAZYWELL OR CLASSENWELL POOL, NEAR SHEEPSTOR.

vings; and the same enrichment, but with a different pattern, will be found on the east side of the chancel portion.

The Screen was brought to Sheepstor on March 3rd and 4th, 1914, by road across Dartmoor from Exeter. God arrayed Dartmoor in white garments to receive the Screen. On both days the moor was covered with deep snow. A month's hard work fixed the screen in its position in the Church.

VIII. 4. **The Well of St. Leonard** is by the roadside opposite the house to the east of the churchyard. This is a very ancient well, and is described in deeds belonging to the parish of the reign of Queen Elizabeth. It was restored in 1910. The waters of many of the Cornish wells were highly valued for their healing properties. In many parishes the water from the Holy Well was always used in the administration of the Sacrament of Holy Baptism   There are no records to show that any value was attached in bygone days to the waters of the Well of St. Leonard, but it is a very ancient and interesting spring.

VIII. 5. **The Bull Ring** was found in August, 1908, in the middle of the Vicarage field, on the south side of the church, embedded eighteen inches below the soil.   Its existence under the turf was discovered by Mr. Amos Shillibeer, who told us that he was ploughing the field one day more than forty years ago, and the point of his plough share caught in the ring and pulled him up very abruptly. We made a prolonged search with crowbars, and eventually his son, Mr. George Shillibeer, came upon it.

It is now raised to the level of the ground, and can easily be seen from the churchyard; and the large granite block to which it is fixed, which is five feet long, is placed in exactly the same position as that in which it was found.

The Bull Ring was formerly used for bull-baiting. The bull was tied to the ring and then baited with dogs. The dogs, which were killed in the fray, were usually buried under the stone which supported the ring.

At these barbarous festivities the women wore peculiar aprons, in which they caught the bull-dog when it was tossed.   The villagers irreverently held their feastings and festivities amongst the tombstones in the churchyard. While a fight was going on, the spectators sat along the churchyard wall and watched the fun, repairing at frequent intervals to the ale-house adjoining the field for refreshment   The old sport has long since died out, but the old ale-house still continued to refresh the thirsty within the memory of some people still living.   Some years ago it was pulled down, with the cottage adjoining, and the building now seen is St. Leonard's Room.

Although bull-baiting was indulged in at Sheepstor in the days of long ago, there is no evidence whatever to support the statement that I have heard made, that prize-fighting was prevalent there.

The Old Vicarage, or Priest's House, adjoins the church-yard, and was built about 1300 and restored in 1658. The date carved in relief on the wall records the restoration.

The Church House, on the south side of the church-yard, is now the Parish Room.

VIII. 6. **The Rajah's Tomb** is under the large beech tree in the churchyard. It is the Mecca of West Country tourists, who go and stare at the tomb without having the least notion of the history of the hero whose memory it perpetuates. Some go so far astray as to think that the famous Rajah was a black man. (See " Rajah Brooke.")

Pixies

Sheepstor itself is traditionally held to be rich in precious metals carefully guarded by pixies, who it would appear are sufficiently niggardly in their habits.

> Little pixy, fair and slim,
> Without a rag to cover him.

The miner hears the tinkle of the pixy hammers in the depths of the mine, but the pixy never offers him any of the golden ore he has extracted. A pixy who visited nightly a farmhouse near Sheepstor, and swept the hearth and did various kind offices for the house, for which he was repaid by a cake left out for him each night, was pitied by the farmer's wife, who peered at him through a chink, because he was so ragged and torn in his apparel, so—in the kindness of her heart—she made him a little suit of broadcloth and laid it in the kitchen for him. When the pixy saw this, away went his tatters, and arraying himself in the new suit he capered about, singing

> Pixy fine and pixy gay,
> Pixy now will run away.

One notion anciently held on the moor, was that the souls of unbaptised babies that had died passed wailing in the wind.

> The wind blows cold on waste and wold,
>   It bloweth night and day ;
> The souls go by 'twixt earth and sky,
>   Impatient, cannot stay.
> They fly in clouds and flap their shrouds,
>   When full the moon doth sail,
> In dead of night, when lacketh light,
>   We hear them pipe and wail.
>
> And many a soul with des'late howl,
>   Doth rattle at the door,
> Or rove and rout, with dance and shout,
>   Around the granite tor.
> We hear a soul 'i th' chimney growl,
>   That's drenched with the rain,
> To wring the wet from winding sheet,
>   And see the fire 'l were fain.

But all this belongs to the past. It is doubtful whether the present generation has heard these stories. If they have they have scouted them as old wives' fables. And yet one hardly knows whether there may not linger on, though unacknowledged, some superstitious ideas imbibed in childhood. I knew a case that occurred not so many years ago when a young carpenter sat up on St. Mark's eve in the church porch. On that eve a watcher there is supposed to see pass by him the forms of those who will die in the parish in the ensuing twelve months. The young man averred most solemnly that he had seen himself pass by into the church. He took to his bed and died. The parson who visited him did his utmost to disabuse him of the idea, told him that a passing light had cast his shadow against the wall. The young carpenter would not be shaken in his conviction, and died, though there was actually nothing but sheer fright to account for his death.

Witchcraft is by no means extinct, nor faith in it, and it is to be feared that it will be a long time before the white witch ceases to be a recipient of money, and a dealer in charms. Here is a remedy which a white witch gave for a sprain :

2 ozs. of oil of turpentine		
2 ,,	,,	earthworms
2 ,,	,,	swillowes (what this is I do not know)
2 ,,	,,	opedildoc

The opedildoc and the turpentine were the sole useful condiments in the composition. But usually the white witch uses verbal charms.

Of course ghosts will hold their own quite as long as the white witch. I am not aware whether any one of the old Elford's " walks " among the ruins of Longstone.

CHAPTER IX.

WALKS AROUND SHEEPSTOR.

1—*Sheep's Tor.* 2—*Round the Tor.* 3—*Nosworthy Bridge* 4—*Crazywell Pool.* 5—*Leather Tor and Peak Hill.* 6— *Nosworthy Bridge and Nillacombe Valley.* 7—*Down Tor.* 8—*Deancombe Valley.* 9—*Eylesbarrow, Nun's Cross to Princetown.* 10—*Broad Rock.*

IX. 1. **Ascent of Sheepstor** (1 mile.) The first effort every visitor with a fairly strong pair of legs sets his mind on is a scramble to the top of Sheep's Tor.

We will therefore start from Sheepstor Cross, and passing through the churchyard proceed up the lane.

Before we leave the church behind us, I should like to mention that Sheepstor Church was the scene of the goose story. Until it was separated from Bickleigh, and endowed by the late Sir Massey Lopes, Sheepstor was only entitled to one service in three weeks. One Sunday morning the Vicar of Bickleigh entered the church to conduct Divine Service, but was entreated by the clerk not to use the pulpit, as his old goose had been sitting a fortnight, and would hatch out before his next visit.

Passing up the lane, a cottage is seen on the left hand, beside the plantation. A farmhouse formerly stood here which had a history.

A thrifty farmer once lived there and saved his money, but in those days there were not the banking facilities there are to-day. One night the house was entered by robbers, who stole £200. They were traced to Plymouth and their house was searched, but no trace of the money could be found. As the police were leaving the house, they noticed a loaf on the table. They lifted it up. The crust came off, and inside were one hundred sovereigns. One robber was caught and hanged.

Continuing this walk, we are soon out on the open moor.

The name of the tor has no reference to sheep, although flocks of sheep often browse on its breezy slopes, but means " steep." The old names of the tor are Shittes Tor and Schittes Tor.

Sheep's Tor is in the midst of a fine hunting country, and is often drawn by the Dartmoor hounds. The dear old tor ne'er looks prettier than it does in the late autumn and early winter, when the hounds with the huntsmen in their scarlet coats sweep across its rocky shoulder, when the whole hillside is redder than a fox with the dead bracken.

Now for the ascent. There are several good ways. The ascent on the **north** side is very rough ; on the **west,** stiff but pleasant ; at the **southern** extremity, none but the foolhardy, would attempt to scale the precipitous rocks. On the east side is a gentle slope, very easily ascended even by the aged and infirm. To ascend the *west* side, one way is to go through Sheepstor, following the road up to the tor until you pass through the gate just beyond the iron cottage. A few yards further on, branch off across the moor from the wall and follow a rough path, which is not very distinct, towards a thorn tree. Another way is to take the green lane which branches off the road opposite Park Inn. After passing through a gate at the end of the lane, a path leads you up to the tor.

The best way to ascend the *east* side is to follow route 14 to the bend of the wall, then proceed eastwards parallel with the wall one hundred yards, then turn round and ascend.

When, breathless, you reach the top, what a panorama lies before you—

> " Where the mountain's spacious breast
> Opens in airy grandeur to the West,"

where the long and rugged lines of the Cornish mountains

form the horizon.   Brown Willy, with its five peaks, can easily be picked out.

The summit of the tor is very extensive.

> " Here at deep midnight by the moon's chill glance,
>   Unearthly forms prolong their viewless dance."

Sheep's Tor is the home of the pixies.   On the S.W. side, among the clitters near a white rock, is the Pixies' Cave.   Here one of the Elford's found refuge when he

Granite Bases of Cheese & Cider Presses

among Longstone ruins. Sheepstor.

From a drawing   *by Mr. H. W. Harding*

fled from Longstone during the Civil Wars.   On the rocks at the southern end of the tor are rock basins, which, however, have been worn through and no longer retain water.   *3, 14, or 7, 14.

IX. 2   **Round Sheepstor** (4 miles).   Turn up the lane facing the inn.   After passing through the gate at the end of the lane, turn to the left.   This path will lead you to the back of the tor, where the scenery is very fine.   After passing through a third gate on to the moor again as you aacend the hill, pass by the rain guage (enclosed in the iron railings). Keep straight on till you come to a wall. Here you come into the track again which will lead you back to Sheepstor.

7, 7A, 7B, 14A, 31, 14.*

IX. 3. **Sheepstor to Nosworthy Bridge.** (2 miles).

There is a very beautiful walk beside Burrator Lake up Longstone Lane. Half a-mile down the lane you come to

*The numbers at the foot of the paragraphs refer to those on the Map in the end of the book.

the ruins of the fine old manor house of Longstone. The name indicates that a Long Stone, or Menhir, once stood near by. As the ruins are approached, notice a large gate socket in a granite post on your right hand. On the north end of the ruins lie a cheese press, a cider press, and an old crazing mill which ground the corn for the

Granite Corn Crazer

LONGSTONE MANOR
SHEEPSTOR

household. In the middle of the field, on the north side of the house, will be noticed a granite platform. This was the old windstrew, or threshing floor, belonging to the manor house. I don't know of another windstrew in England.

THE WINDSTREW, SHEEPSTOR.

Longstone House has had a great history, and was for generations the seat of the Elford's, who were a powerful family in the sixteenth and seventeenth centuries.

Continuing one's walk along the lane, where the hedge comes to an end, some old millstones may be seen inside the wire fence on the left. These were taken from Sir Francis Drake's old mill, which formerly stood near by, before the Reservoir was formed.

Continuing one's walk, the head of the Reservoir is soon reached. Then follow the new road. This will bring you to Nosworthy Bridge, one of the beauty spots of Dartmoor. Some little distance along the road, which runs between wire fences, the view of Leather Tor is very fine, and reminds one very much of the Matter horn from Zermatt, without its snows.

You can return to Dousland Station by Lowery.

7, 8A, 21A, 21, 40.

IX. 4. **Sheepstor to Crazywell Pool** ($3\frac{1}{2}$ miles).

Route same as (3) to Nosworthy Bridge; but just before reaching the bridge, turn up a footpath to the right, through the ruins of Nosworthy Farm. The path leads you to the road above Kingset. Among the trees North of these ruins, by the river side, lie several fine slag pounding hollows used by the tinners (about 17 hollows). When you reach the road above Kingset Farm, keep on till you come to a gate which leads you out on to the moor, then keep straight on along the track, passing by a gate on your right below. Keep on this rough track about 300 yards, till you come upon a little stream which runs across the road. This stream comes out of the pool.

Turn up to the left and follow the stream between its steep banks—quite a little gorge. As you approach the pool, a high bank faces you, through which the stream filters. Now cross this bank, and you find yourself at the brink of the pool.

So many people experience difficulty in finding it, but if these directions are followed it will be easily found.

The pool is one of the nine wonders of Dartmoor. In the middle is an old mine shaft, which is of great depth, and the bottom has never been fathomed. In 1844 the Devonport municipal authorities were perplexed by a shortage of their water supply, through a prolonged drought. Relying on the fathomless depth of the pool, they set to work to pump the water out and supply the town. The pool was drained, but not the shaft, and just at the critical moment someone claimed the owner-ship of the water, and the work ceased and the weird old pool was allowed to retain its secret, and is likely to do so for many a year to come.

It is said that voices are heard at the pool, calling by

name the next person who would die in the parish. The
sounds are caused by the wind as it swirls over the water.

About 30 yards N. of the pool are the remains of a
stone circle, and 100 yards N.E. is a ford by which the
Devonport leat may be crossed,

You can return to Dousland by Leather Tor Bridge and
Lowery.

7, 8, 8B, 21C.   21B, 21A, 21, 40.

IX. 5. Ascent of Leather Tor and Peak Hill (3 miles).

Follow Longstone Lane as far as the head of the
Reservoir. Here follow the new road to Vineylake. Leave
the farm on your right, pass it on its North side, and
cross the road, and begin the ascent. Ascend about half-
way between the two tors, after the wall on your left ends.
Visit the Peak Hill antiquities and return to Dousland by
the Princetown road.

7, 8C.   40.

IX. 6. Sheepstor to Nosworthy Bridge and Nillacombe Valley.

Follow Longstone Lane, and keep to the road
which bears to the L.. this will bring you to Nosworthy
Bridge. The Nillacombe Valley may be ascended by a
rough path which turns off to the L. as you enter the
road to Deancombe. This valley is the roughest of the
rough   The hand of man and the forces of nature have
combined to throw the valley into confusion. Its whole
length is strewn with stream works. Above Kingset the
Nillacombe flows through a small but wild gorge, strewn
with boulders, and the heaps and pits left by the tinners.
Beyond the head of the valley, Siward's Cross is quite
near.

IX. 7. Sheepstor to Down Tor Stone Circle and Stone Row (4 m.)

Follow Langstone Lane nearly to Nosworthy
Bridge, then turn sharply to the right. Pass the ruins of
Middleworth Farm, up to Deancombe Farm ruin. From
thence there are two ways. From Deancombe Farm
follow up the green lane on the west side of the farm
which leads up to Down Tor. You soon find yourself on
the moor. Follow the wall till it takes a sharp turn to
the right, then strike south-east, and in about fifty yards

you come upon a cart track which leads you right by the remains

The other way, which I always think is by far the pleasanter, is by Combeshead Farm. If this latter be taken, the Stone Row and Circle show to much greater advantage, when they come into view. The following directions will make the way clear. Just before reaching Deancombe

DOWN TOR CIRCLE AND STONE ROW.

Farm, turn down the lane to the right and cross the Dean, and then take the path up the valley to Combeshead Farm. Or you can go through Deancombe Farm and take the footpath up ro Combeshead Farm. On reaching the farm, pass through a gate below the farm. You then soon find yourself on an old cart track.

Follow this track across the shoulder of the tor, to a wall. You will see a gate in the wall. After passing through the gate, the Stone Row and Circle stand up against the skyline—a noble monument.

The stones were tampered with in 1880, but the late Rev. S. Baring-Gould and the late Mr Robert Burnard came to the rescue and saved this beautiful monument from destruction, in the same way as they have saved so many.

By kind permission of the]   *[Western Morning News*

A MOORMAN's FUNERAL — of William Pengelly, aged 90 — of Combeshead, in 1932.

They repaired the damage done and re-erected the fallen stones.

The Circle, which is 42 ft. in diameter, and contains 24 stones, and formerly enclosed a large kistvaen. The row is 1,175 ft. long, and it continues up to the tumulus, but the stones at this end are smaller and nearly all are under the turf. Note the tumulus on the N. side of the circle.

From the tumulus at the east end of the row, Nun's Cross Farm is very accessible. Looking eastward, you see a dip in the hills ; the farm lies in a line with this dip, not more than 200 yards. on the other side.

As you approach the farm, look to the left and you see Siward's Cross standing by the hedge at the N.W. side of the new take.

From the farm you can journey on to Princetown, or back to Sheepstor *via* Eylesbarrow ; either way provides splendid moorland scenery.

On the W. side of Down Tor, about 40 yds. above the wall, is a shelter formed by a hugh projecting boulder. One may shelter here from a passing shower.

7, 8, 35 ; or 7, 8, 32, 33, 34 ; or 7, 8, 30, 34.

From Nun's Cross is a magnificient view, which is at its best when the gorse or the heather is out in bloom. In the distance, eastward are the heights above Dartmeet, and northward the fine tors below which the East and West Dart flow – a splendid background to a fine sweep of country. On a bright afternoon in August the view is hard to beat.

Nun's Cross is one of a long line of crosses which formerly stretched from Buckfastleigh Abbey to Buckland Abbey, and marked the track across the moor used by the monks. This is not the Abbot's Way, which lies further to the south. Two more of these crosses will be found within the new-take of the ruined Farm at Fox Tor. Another has been found a little to the S.E. of Nun's Cross Farm. Two more on the moor to the N.W. of Nun's Cross, above Kingset, which we re-erected.

Another stands at the wall by the roadside just above Vinneylake Farm, and another outside the gate on the green opposite Lowery Farm. A base of another lies by a gate on the N. side of the Princetown road, about a $\frac{1}{4}$ m. E. of Dousland Station.

IX. 8. **Sheepstor to Deancombe Valley.** One of the most charming walks from Sheepstor is over the southern shoulder of the tor into the Deancombe Valley.

Follow the track along the wall above Yellowmeade. When the wall goes no further, keep straight on and strike the wall in front. Then follow this wall over a stream, and keep to it till the track passes through a gate into a grassy field with several large boulders in it. Then descend into the valley. The view down the valley is exceedingly fine.

Ascending the opposite hill—

> " Above, beneath. immensely spread,
> Valleys and hoary rocks I view."

The view from the top of Down Tor is hardly beaten on Dartmoor.   3, 14, 41.

IX. 9. **Sheepstor to Eylesbarrow** (4 m., time 1 hour), **and Nun's Cross** (7 m.) **and Princetown** (11 m.) To Burracombe Gate (II), and then follow the track up to the mine buildings. Soon after passing these buildings there is a fork in the track; take the track to the L. and follow it on to Nun's Cross and Princetown. About 200 yds. N. of the mine Buildings are two fine tumuli close together. The view from the further one is the very finest in this quarter of the moor.

3, 4, 5, 6.

IX. 10. **Sheepstor to Broad Rock.** Same as IX. 9 as far as Eylesbarrow mine buildings. At the fork in the track referred to above keep straight on. You soon come to a dip in the hills, where are the ruins of a house. On your left hand is a delightful spring of water which gushes forth from a veritable subterranean reservoir.

The pond from which it springs is of great depth, probably an old mine shaft. There is no purer water on Dartmoor. The combe below is Evil Combe.

Continuing one's walk along the cart track, you soon come on to the upper waters of the Plym, which the track crosses at Abbot's Ford, and here you are on the old Abbot's Way. There are several great trackways across the Darmoor desert. There is *Fur Tor Cut* which passes Fur Tor—a cattle drive used by moormen to move the cattle from one place to another. *The Abbot's Way* connects the Abbey of Buckfastleigh with Tavistock and Buckland Abbeys. *The Sandy Way* is a very ancient trackway which crosses the moor E. to W., which passed across Fox Tot, Down Ridge, Lowery and Dousland ; it is marked by crosses. *The Lych Way* was a track over which the bodies of moormen who had died on the moor were carried to their burial at Lydford.

(For Plym Head from Abbot's Ford follow the river to its source). After crossing the river, steer S.E., and about 1 m. further on you will see a pole standing up with a notice board fixed to it. This is Broad Rock—the Cranmere of the southern quarter of the moor. All around is very boggy ground, although no danger exists for those who will use ordinary common sense.

From this high and boggy land the inhabitants of Sheepstor secure their peat for fuel, &c.

If you steer S.W. you come to Langcombe Kistvaen in the valley of that name. Thence you can return by Ditsworthy to Sheepstor.

Or from Broad Road, Plym Head lies about 1 m. due N., but the ground is very swampy for a good part of the way.

As you approach Plym Head the ground is firm, and it is a pleasant walk down the Plym to Abbot's Ford, which is crossed to go to Broad Rock.

IX. 11. **Yellowmead Circles.** The existence of the fine prehistoric stone monument, which the megalithic circles on Yellowmead Down, Sheepstor form, was unknown until 1921, and is the greatest discovery of recent years on Dartmoor. The honour of the discovery rests with Mr. R. Hansford Worth, whose skilled eye noted the humps formed by the stones which were lying prostrate under

Photos by]   Yellowmead Circles.   [*Mr. R. Hansford Worth*

the turf which formed the outer circle, of which only one large stone and two small ones were standing, and he expressed the opinion that it was probably a double circle.

That they had escaped detection so long was due in some measure to the fact that they had for many years been covered with a very high growth of heather ; this was burnt a year or so before Mr. Worth made his discovery. Owing to the prolonged drought of the 1921 summer, I

Photo by]   YELLOWMEAD CIRCLES.   *[R Hansford Worth*

noticed that there were many patches of whortleberry scrubs and grass which were burnt up inside the large circle, which indicated the presence of stones buried not far under the surface.

FOUR CONCENTRIC CIRCLES.

In the autumn of 1921, on behalf of the Dartmoor Preservation Society, Mr. William Manning, of Yellowmead Farm, close by, and I, with the assistance of others, took in hand the task of unearthing these buried stones

D

and re-erecting them in their old socket holes. It proved a formidable task, for we found instead of one circle that there were four concentric circles.

Of these four circles the outer circle is composed of large stones, many of them slabs about 4 ft. by 6 ft. It is very incomplete, as some of the stones have been taken away and built into the newtake wall of Yellowmead Farm, about 100 yards to the west. The depressions in the ground show that large stones have evidently been removed from the north east arc; these have probably been removed to form the small bridge across the streamlet in the gully 200 yards north-west of the circle. The three stones which form this bridge have such a strong likeness to the other slabs which form the outer circle, that their origin can hardly be doubted. This outer circle consists now of 24 stones, and has a diameter of 66 ft. Some of the small stones in the west arc may be only triggers of much larger stones which have been taken away to build the wall. The largest stone in the south-east arc was 5 ft. 6 in. as it lay on the ground, but is now 4 ft. 3 in. high. It has on its top two or three depressions which have the appearance of cup markings. It bears remarkable resemblance to the largest stone in the Brisworthy Circle; its height is the same, and its girth near the bottom is also of the same measurement.

The second circle consists of 28 stones, and has a diameter of 50ft. It is composed of smaller stones, which are placed with marked regularity on the east and south sides.

The third circle consists of 31 small stones, and has a diameter of 37ft.

The fourth and innermost circle consists of 21 stones, and has a diameter of 22 ft. It is composed of thick ponderous stones. This enclosed either a kistvaen, of which no trace remains, or a large cairn, of which there are still indications. It encircled the burial-place of some king or powerful chief of pre-historic times. The Dartmoor Preservation Society intends to excavate this inner platform in the hope of finding an urn.

These four concentric circles are, therefore, composed of no less than 104 stones, and the whole monument consists of 118 stones.

THE OUTSTANDING STONES.

On the west side are 14 stones, which have formed the beginnings of probably as many as eight or nine stone rows running parallel in a westerly direction. These have all been destroyed to build the newtake wall, although on the way they are still traceable. The largest of these stones close ro the circle is trigged up by a large natural boulder which is buried underground. About 161 ft. east of the circle are the remains of a small barrow which has been contained by a small circle of stones, four of which remain, and which has a diameter of 10 ft.

About 80 yards further east is a large slab about $5\frac{1}{2}$ ft. square Connected with it are two or three stones which have formerly stood erect. About 130 yards north east of the circles is a fallen mennir, 6 ft. 3 in. long; connected with it are three stones running in a south-easterly direction.

HOW TO REACH THE CIRCLES.

After passing through Sheepstor turn to the left and go up the lane towards the tor. After passing through the gate on to the open moor follow the road until you come to another gate. Enter this and follow the green lane until you come to the open moor again ; here turn to the right towards the fir trees; the circles are on the east side of these. As you cross the gully on to the open moor, the three stones spanning the streamlet of which I have spoken will be crossed.

The leat course which runs along the west side of the circles discharged itself into the gully about 50 yards above this bridge for the purpose of turning the water wheel of a blowing house which formerly stood there, and of which, now not a single trace remains except the leat.

CHAPTER X.
DOUSLAND.

Photo by]　　　　　　　　　[*Mr. R. Hansford Worth.*
TIN MOULD AT COLYTON, SHEEPSTOR.

FOR all who desire a place conveniently situated, where they may enjoy the bracing moorland air, and at the same time have a very convenient centre for excursions, Yelverton and Dousland offer unrivalled facilities.

When staying on the moor it is a great advantage to be near a railway station, and Yelverton and Dousland each has one in its midst. Yelverton and Dousland as centres for Dartmoor excursions are second to none. If one's excursions are carefully planned, one can visit every place of interest in the western and southern portions of the moor.

The following excursions will be much appreciated by all who love the beauties of nature, whose kindly hand has lavished her gifts and her charms on Dartmoor.

MEAVY.

X. I. **Dousland to Sheepstor** (2 m.) A very pleasant walk. After leaving the station, turn to the R. and cross the railway. In less than $\frac{1}{4}$ m. you reach Prowse's Crossing. At this point two routes are open to you. Either keep straight on and take the first turning to the L., or turn up to the L., cross the railway, and take the path across the down, which branches off in a southerly direction. Either way is extremely beautiful, and will lead you to Burrator Bridge. The waterfall at the bridge is very grand after much rain.

For Sheepstor cross the bridge.

Go one way and return the other.   Or on your return to the bridge from Sheepstor, you can turn to the R. and return to Dousland by the old lane past the plantation.

1, 1A, 2. | 2, 1. | 2, 21, 40.

X. 2. **Dousland to Meavy** (1 m.) Start in the same way as walk X. 1. but turn neither to the right hand nor to the left until you descend the hill.   At this point in the road turn to the R.   Meavy is in the valley.

A prettier village green you never saw, with its stately cross, its old-world village inn, and its venerable church in the background.

> " And in the midst an oak whose woven boughs display
>   A verdant canopy of light and shade ;
>   Throned on a rock its giant form appears,
>   In the full manhood of eight hundred years."

Under its shade in " ye olden days " the old fiddler sat and fiddled the pretty tunes of the old country dances, while the villagers danced on the green.

1, 38, 39.

The church has a fine reredos, and a curious capital in the chancel arch, which is Norman. It also has some good stained glass and a beautifully mellow peal of six bells. It formerly possessed a fine screen, but this was destroyed in 1840, and the church despoiled of much that was beautiful. The only indication now of a screen is the rood loft door behind the pulpit. There is a good waggon roof with excellent bosses.

There is a pretty walk to Sheepstor from Meavy by the side of the leat through the wood. For this, turn into the field beside the blacksmith's shop opposite the School. On the school is a replica of Drake's Drum which summons the children to school daily.

The Village Cross. This fine octagonal cross was replaced in its present position by the Rev, W. A. G. Gray, rector for many years. He found the shaft buried up in the churchyard wall; it was set up again on August 24th, 1893, by the rector, Mr. Gray, who was assisted in the work by Fred Creber, Jack Bickle and Richard Bickle.

X. 3. Dousland to Vixen Tor and Merrivale Bridge (5 m.) After leaving the station, turn to the L. and pass through Walkhampton to Huckworthy Bridge, which is very picturesque.

Huckworthy Hill is very steep. Soon after reaching the top, you will come to cross roads. Then turn to the R. and keep on this road, passing Sampford Spiney Church.

After passing through a gate, you are on the moor again, with Pew Tor in front of you. It is the road to the R. you are wanting. After passing through another gate, you enter the Vale of the Walkham. The drive up this valley in May, when the larches are putting on their spring garments and the hillsides are gorgeously apparelled with the furze bloom, is exquisitely beautiful. About a mile further on, Vixen Tor is reached; an ideal place for a picnic.

It is a short mile from here to Merrivale Bridge. About 100 yards north of the Tor is a kistvaen. First you come to a standing stone, which has been connected with it. Get the trees in the wall in a line with this stone and you will pass right by the kistvaen, which has its cover stone and a containing circle of stones. It was discovered by Dr. A. E. H. Tutton, on August 1st, 1916.

The view from the field to S.W. of the tor, looking E. over the cottage, with the hill in the background golden with furze bloom, is superb.

41, 42, 43, 44, 45, 46, 47.

There is no road between Vixen Tor and Merrivale Bridge, but the pedestrian has two alternate routes by which he can return.

Either turn down the road on the R. after crossing Merrivale Bridge. 50, 49, 48, 42, 41.

Or, by following the Tavistock road, and turning to the L. at the Moor Shop, where a fine octagonal cross with one arm will be seen, which I found in March, 1909.

60, 54, 53, 51, 43, 42, 41.

Visitors to Vixen Tor, please don't strew the ground with paper and broken bottles, which gives great annoyance to the owner.

X. 4. Dousland to Peak Hill Circle and Stone Rows. Follow the Princetown road to the pond at the top of the hill.

The stone row, which starts from a cairn, passes through the south end of the pond, and terminates some distance below in a small circle of seven stones.   About 320 yds. due east of the circle, and only 40 yds. from the road, is another stone row which has been mutilated.   It is only about 30 yds. long, and starts from a ruined circle.

X. 5. Dousland to Lowery Tor, Sharpitor and Leather Tor. Take the Princetown road, and after passing through the railway arch *above* the plantation on the R. take to the moor and ascend Peak Hill. Lowery Tor is the highest point of Peak Hill, and from it an excellent view of the Meavy Valley and Burrator Lake is obtained.   Near the tor, on its W. side, is a large dilapidated cairn.

Proceeding on to Sharpitor Tor, a little to the R. is the beautiful cone of Leather Tor, which is very easily ascended from its N. side.   The E. and S. sides are covered with some of the most remarkable clitters of rocks on the moor.   Descend either by the footpath on the S.W. which leads to Vineylake, or on the N. side and follow the wall, which runs along below the tor, to the road which leads to Leather Tor Farm.   Nosworthy Bridge, which spans the Meavy, will be seen in the valley below.

X. 6. Dousland to Black Tor Antiquities.   Continue walk (X. 4) to the bottom of the hill, and at the bend of the road beyond is a green road which leads to Stanlake. Keep on the Princetown road beyond this road to the bottom of the next hill. Then take to the moor, and strike the wall to the E. On the E. side of this wall runs a **very fine stone row**, which has been robbed to build the wall, but there is still a very good row left, and it

VIXEN TOR.

ends in a very substantial blocking·stone at its N. end; apparently it was a double row, and one of the rows is buried in the wall for support.

Mr. Baring-Gould told me that a very fine kistvaen once stood near here on the W. of Black Tor, but it was destroyed by the road menders.

Harter Tor stone rows can be seen from the tor on the opposite side of the Meavy, running down to the river.

They consist of two fine rows. One is mutilated, but

they terminate in circles which formerly enclosed cairns.

An old tinner's blowing house is down below by the river side.

X. 7. **Leat Falls.** Continuing one's walk from where walk (6) terminated, a torrent rushes down from the moor in a succession of cascades just below the stone rows, and joins the Meavy. It is a beautiful spot.

Lower down are the Leat falls, where the Devonport leat comes tumbling and foaming down the hillside in a fine cascade, before it crosses the river through the acqueduct.

X. 8. **Nosworthy Bridge** is reached by Lowery.

40, 21, 21A, 8A.

The walk may be continued to Deancombe and Down Tor.

X. 9. **Round Leather Tor.** After passing Lowery cottage the road forks to the right. It leads to Nosworthy Bridge. To the left to Leather Tor Farm. Follow the road to the left till the leat crosses the road. Then follow the leat up for some distance and leave it where it enters a field ; here take the wall as your guide and rejoin the Princetown road, but keep on the high ground and visit the very fine hut circles on N.E. slopes of Sharpitor.

The brawling leat above Leather Tor Farm, with the tor in the background, presents a fine piece of mountain scenery.   40, 21, 21A.   40.

X. 10. **Crazywell Pool.** *Via* Lowery and Leather Tor Bridge.

40, 21, 21A, 21B, 21C.   8B, 8, 7, 2, 1.

X. 11. **Brisworthy Circle.** *Via* Marchant's Cross and Lynch Hill.

1, 39A, 11, 21, 22.

I cannot conclude these brief notes of Sheepstor without putting in a plea for the preservation of the ferns. Let the visitor if he will carry away bunches of the pink heath and heather, even the luck bearing white heather, if he can find it ; handfuls of golden water marigold —*drunkards* the people call them, though they drink water only—wild roses, if they do not mind scratching their fingers; the pretty little marsh violet, the round-leafed sundew, the broom, the golden saxifrage, the pretty luck-bean and the field gentian, but let them spare the ferns that they tear up by the roots. *Osmunda regalis* once grew by the streams, throwing its fronds six feet high—now it is utterly eradicated. The two *Hymenophylla*, once so abundant in the Plym upper valley and in the roads near Meavy, can now scarcely be met with; the little oak fern is extremely rare. They are torn up and carried away—to die.

CONVICT PRISON, PRINCETOWN.

CHAPTER XI.

PRINCETOWN.

1—*Ingra Tor.* 2—*Merrivale.* 3—*Vixen Tor.* 4—*Staple and Cox Tors.* 5—*Great and Fur Tors.* 6—*Nun's Cross.* 7—*Fox Tor and Child's Tomb.* 8—*Crazywell Pool.* 9—*Nillacombe Valley.* 10—*Leather Tor.*

Princetown is the highest town in England and stands 1,400 ft. above sea level, near the base of North Hessary Tor. The air is very bracing and invigorating. It is a very good centre for exploring the moor, especially for motorists, as the roads are excellent. They will find most comfortable head-quarters at the Duchy Hotel, which is very up-to-date and exceedingly well managed. The King and Queen stayed here a few days, when, as Prince and Princess of Wales they visited their tenants in the Duchy in June, 1910.

The Prison. The great convict prison which our fellow-countrymen all over the land associate with Dartmoor, was built very early in the nineteenth century. The foundation stone was laid on March 20th, 1806, and the buildings were very quickly erected. It was built for a military prison, and it was soon crowded to overflowing with prisoners of war, of whom the greater number were Frenchmen, captured during the great war with Napoleon which closed with his defeat at Waterloo. The prisoners loudly complained about the severity of the Dartmoor winter; and no wonder, for many of them had the misfortune to be securely lodged in Dartmoor prison during the greatest frost England has experienced in modern times—which continued with great persistency during the first three months of 1814. Escapes are now rare.

An assize has recently been concluded at Princetown and 23 convicts sentenced for various periods for mutiny.

XI. 1. **To Peak Hill and Ingra Tor.** Take the Plymouth road. 2 m. from Princetown a very fine piece of mountain scenery lies before you. The tors on L. of the road are Sheep's Tor, Leather Tor and Sharpitor. Ascending Peak Hill, L. is a road to Stanlake Farm in Meavy Valley. R. are some roadmen's stone quarries and heaps. Here turn R. and cross the moor for Leeden Tor. Either cross the tor or make your way along its western slopes for Ingra Tor. About 300 yds. E. of Ingra Tor is a fine kistvaen which has not been disturbed, except that a portion of the capstone has been broken off. This old monument is known to very few people. It was originally covered by a mound, as so many are, a portion of which still remains.

From Ingra Tor the Walkham Valley is most picturesque. In the autumn the foliage of the Walkham Woods is gorgeous.

Cross the railway E. of Ingra Tor; then cross the little valley and pass over the railway crossing at the foot of King Tor. The Halt is here. Beyond the railway is a path which leads back to Princetown

XI. 2. **Merrivale Bridge** (3 m.) Either by the Tavistock road, or strike across the moor from the station, across the shoulder of N. Hessary Tor. It is a rough walk across the moor, as there is no track, but it is well worth the extra effort. A little stream with huge boulders in its course is struck $1\frac{1}{2}$ m. from the tor. Thence ascend the rising ground and the antiquities are in front of you.

MERRIVALE BRIDGE.

Merrivale Avenues consist of two long stone rows. They run E. and W. parallel to each other, 105 ft. apart, the longest 1,143 ft. and the other nearly 800 ft. The former has the remains of a circle in the centre.

Merrivale Kistvaen is a very large one. The capstone was mutilated by a farmer in 1860, who cut a gate post out of the middle of it.

Merrivale Longstone is seen S.W. of the Avenues and is 12 ft. high. It is a conspicuous object in the distance A smaller menhir is near by.

Merrivale Circle, a small circle with 8 stones, close to the Longstone. It formerly enclosed a kistvaen. Its diameter is 67 ft. These remains and others close by suffered severely when the new-take wall was built.

The Apple-crusher will be found among the hut circles. It is a circular stone cut out ready for use in the cider press, but it was never removed.

The Prehistoric Village lies between the road and the avenues. Many of the hut dwellings are large and well preserved. This group of hut circles is known locally as the *Plague Market*. Here, when Tavistock was being ravaged by the plague in 1625, in which year its mortality rose to 575, the farmers brought provisions and placed them for the people of Tavistock to take away, who left money in payment for the produce received at an appointed place. The same thing was done at Eyam in Derbyshire in 1665.

The huts were built by courses of stones placed one above another. The roof was formed by poles thatched over At the point where the poles converged, a cap was fitted in made of a hollowed stone. Specimens of these stones have occasionally been found. The doorway was formed by two jambs with a lintel. The latter are frequently still in position.

As one descends the road towards the bridge, below the 5 milestone the road makes a bend. Here a foot-track cuts across the moor and rejoins the road below. This passes through the groups of hut circles. From the antiquities descend to the bridge.

Merrivale Bridge is comparatively new. The old clapper bridge was swept away in a great flood during a thunderstorm in July, 1890. This storm caused freshets in several of the Dartmoor streams and carried away many bridges. There was a memorable flood at Peter Tavy on that occasion. A stroll up the Walkham is very pleasant; there are three Blowing Houses on the E. side of the stream. It is a fine trout stream. The fishing rights belong to the Dartmoor Angling Association.

XI. 3 **Vixen Tor** is the fine pile of rocks on the L. above the Walkham Valley. It will be unwise to attempt to reach it by a short cut from the bridge, as the ground is very swampy.

LANGSTONE CIRCLE.

Ascend the hill past the quarries. When the top of the hill has been gained, a footpath branches off to the L. towards the tor and runs parallel with a new-take wall.

The tor is the private property of Mr. Parsons, who lives in the house at the foot of the tor. It has been owned by his family for 200 years. He kindly allows visitors to visit the tor. Of late years so much trouble has been given by thoughtless people, who strew the ground around the tor with paper and broken bottles, that closing the tor to visitors and picnic parties has been under consideration.

The writer pleads with all sorts and conditions of visitors not to leave bottles and refuse about the tor, but to respect the owner's rights, so that no restrictions on the present privileges the public enjoy may be necessary. Do as you would be done by.

Vixen Tor Kistvaen will be found on the N. of the tor near the wall; it is 4 ft. by 1 ft. 9 in. One side stone is 5 ft. in length.

XI. 4. **Great Staple Tor.** There is a lane just above the inn which turns up to Shillapark Farm. Follow this a short distance, then strike across the moor for the tor, or keep to the Tavistock road to the top of the hill, and then branch off across the moor to the tors.

SWINCOMBE FARM.

The first tor approached is **Little Staple Tor.** Next comes **Middle Staple Tor,** and about $\frac{1}{2}$ m. further on is **Great Staple Tor.** On Great Staple Tor the rocks have weathered into strange shapes. There is a tolmen on this tor.

The eminence westward across the boggy valley is **Cox Tor,** on which are several cairns. Nearly 400 yds. N. of the summit is a very large one. 200 yds. N.N.W. of this one are two very curious ring cairns; one has a diameter of 55 ft. and the other 27 ft. On the S. slope of the tor, 200 ft. below the summit, there is a cluster of small cairns.

Roos Tor formerly was crowned by a fine logan rock, which was mischievously destroyed by quarrymen a generation ago.

From Roos Tor are two very pleasant routes for returning. *Either* steer N.W. and strike the delightful coombe of Peter Tavy, down which the Peter Tavy Brook rushes and babbles over its rocky bed as it hurries on its way to meet the Tavy.

About 1 m. from Roos Tor are clusters of prehistoric huts, which have formed quite a little town ; *or* from the tor steer N.E. on to Langstone Moor, where **The Langstone** keeps its solitary watch over the plain. It is 12 ft. high. The Langstone was formerly the end of a stone row, composed of quite small stones, running in a direction N. and S. from a pool that occupies the site of a destroyed cairn. Nearly parallel to it, and 60 yds. away, was another row. The stone is composed of local gabbro, and was formerly prostrate, but His Grace the Duke of Bedford has re-erected it in its original socket-hole. The old lych way ran from Whittenburrow to it, and then passed on to Cudlip Town.

Looking E. from the Langstone, about $\frac{1}{2}$ m. distant will be seen the **Langstone Circle,** which is a fine specimen of this class of monument, which I have explained in my book on the Land's End (No. 5, pp. 89-91). It was discovered as recently as 1894. Not a single stone was then standing, but fortunately none had been taken away or even mutilated. The Duke of Bedford kindly allowed the stones to be re-erected, and supplied the men to do the work, which was directed by the late Rev. S. Baring-Gould and the late Mr. Robert Burnard. It has 16 stones, and its diameter is about 60 ft. There was originally another circle outside this one, of which only two or three stones remain.

From the circle one can cross the Walkham by Greenaball to Mis Tor, and from there return to Princetown.

XI. 5. **Great Mis Tor** is a very easy excursion from Princetown. Take the Tavistock road to Rundlestone, then turn up the rough road to the R. by the cottages.

Here a wall is your companion for some distance; when it parts company with you, strike for the tor. **Fice's Well,** which bears the date 1568, is now within the prison lands. On the E. side of the prison leat is the new-take wall of the prison farm, running N. and S. The well is over the wall, close to that portion of the wall which runs in an E. direction.

Photo by]   *[R. Hansford Worth.*
Re-erecting Brisworthy Circle.—*See page* 23.

Beardown Clapper Bridge, Beardown Man on Devil Tor, and Wistman's Wood I have described in my chapter on Two Bridges (No. 2, IX. 3-9). At Mis Tor is Mis Tor Pan.

It is only a short distance from Great Mis Tor to **Fur Tor** (1,877 ft.), an island of firm ground rising in the midst of a sea of almost impassable bogs, through which Fur Tor Cut passes, which is the way across the bogs used by moormen for removing their cattle.

XI. 6. **Nun's Cross Farm.** *Either* take the road past Tor Royal, and at the point where it turns L. to White-works, take the rough track which runs nearly due S.; *or* take the path behind the "Plume of Feathers" which leads to South Hessary Tor, whence keep on the ridge which trends S.S.E. Nun's Cross will be found where this ridge ends. It is situated on a neck of land which separates the Nillacombe and Swincombe Valleys.

On the W. side of the new-take wall is Nun's Cross, which was one of a long line of crosses which marked the monks' trackway connecting Buckfastleigh with Buckfast Abbey. It bears the inscriptions: *Crux Siwardi*; *Bocland*. The cross was thrown down and broken 90 years ago, but the late Sir Ralph Lopes, in 1846, took compassion on the fractured and prostrate form of this symbol of the Faith and had it mended and re-erected.

One can proceed on to Eylesbarrow. From the cairns on the highest point is one of the finest views in the Southern Quarter. On reaching the ruined building of the old mine, turn to the R., follow the track, and return by Sheepstor to Dousland Station.

The distance from Princetown to Nun's Cross, Eyles-barrow, Sheepstor and Dousland is 11 m.

XI. 7. **Fox Tor and Child's Tomb** (1 m. E. of Nun's Cross). Fox Tor is not a conspicuous tor. It crowns a rugged elongated hill which stretches down to Fox Tor Mire, a very formidable swamp, where one of the few escapes from Princetown disappeared and was never heard of again. There is a safe path across the mire from Fox Tor to Whiteworks. The low bank which is seen winding

across the flat ground from the white gate below the tor
marks it.

When I was approaching Child's Tomb one day in
May, 1912, the largest fox that I have ever seen on Dartmoor sprang up out of the heather, and after leaping
across the wall, it ran leisurely over the top of Fox Tor.

Fox Tor Brook is a delightful torrent which takes its
rise in Cater's Beam and flows among the rocks on the
highest ground of Fox Tor, and descends into the Swin-

Fox Tor Mire.

combe Valley in a succession of small but charming
cascades.

A Ruined Kistvaen. About 1 m. E. of Nun's Cross Farm,
on the W. side of the dip formed by a lateral stream of
the Swincombe, are the remains of this kistvaen. A block
of white spa will be seen in the wall which is one's companion from Nun's Cross to Fox Tor. The kistvaen lies
about 60 yds. S.E. of the white spa, and about 45 yds. in
a direct line from the wall.

Child's Tomb. Looking down from Fox Tor are two
little depressions, through which flow streamlets—feeders
of the Swincombe—which unite before reaching the latter.

On the little ridge which separates these streams, about

half-way between them, and a $\frac{1}{4}$ m. due N. of the Tor, is Child's Tomb. It is the ruin of a kistvaen. Connected with it is the well-known legend of Child the Hunter, who must have lived at Plymstock before the Norman Conquest, because in the Domesday Book the lands in Plymstock are recorded as belonging to the Abbey of Tavistock. The story probably refers to a much earlier legend, and is an instance of those strange legends which are sometimes met with. The Welsh legend of Llewellyn's hound is another instance, which finds its counterpart in other lands.

The story of Child is that his horse became stogged in Fox Tor Mire, and he was overtaken by a snowstorm and perished on the moor. Before he died, he killed his horse and crept inside the animal for warmth, and wrote his will in the animal's blood :

> "The first that finds and brings me to my grave,
> My lands in Plymstock they shall have."

The monks of Tavistock, greedy of gain, hearing of the last will and testament of Child, started at once for the moor and found his lifeless body. On returning to the town, they heard that the monks of Plymstock were waiting at a ford to intercept them. The wily monks changed their course and threw a bridge across the river near the abbey, known to this day as Guile Bridge, and reached the abbey in safety, and gained possession of the lands in Plymstock.

XI. 8. **Crazywell Pool** is 3 m. S. of Princetown (No. 1. V. 4). The most direct way is to go to Cramber Tor. There is a delightful walk from Cramber Tor to Down Tor, Deancombe and the Drizzlecombe Antiquities—

> " O'er the rills and the crags and the hills."

The course from Cramber should be set due S. The beautiful valleys of the Nillacombe and Dean are crossed. The pedestrian should return through Sheepstor to Dousland Station. From Cramber Tor the Pool is a short mile distant S.S.W. Keep well up because of the swampy valley. The Devonport leat runs above the Pool, and should be crossed by a footbridge which will be found quite near the Pool.

Another route, if one wants a longer walk, is to follow the rough road to Whiteworks, and then to take the rough cart track which branches off to R. and runs just above Kingset. On this mountain track one may often see—

> " A flock of sheep that leisurely pass by,
> One after another."

In the valley below flows the Nillacombe, or Newley-combe. Through the combe beyond Down Tor is the Dean, which is mentioned in a charter of Isabella de Fortibus, dated 1291 :

> " Still glides the stream, and shall for ever glide ;
> The form remains, the function never dies "

FALLS ON THE MEAVY BELOW BLACK TOR.

XI. 9. **The Nilla-combe Valley.** From Nosworthy Bridge *either* take the green lane up to Kingset and from there descend into the valley, *or* follow up the Nilla-combe, which joins the Meavy below the bridge. It is a rocky valley, but higher up the stream, beyond Kingset, are peeps of great beauty. All the way up the ground has been turned over and over by the tin-streamers, whose heaps of refuse are seen everywhere.

The Nillacombe takes its rise in quite a small spring at the head of the valley, but—

> " Large streams from little fountains flow."

and a little trickle soon expands into a brawling stream.

XI. 10. **Leather Tor and Nosworthy Bridge** ($4\frac{1}{2}$ m.) Take the Plymouth road to the point where the road goes down to Stanlake Farm. Here branch off across the moor, keeping Leather Tor on your R. hand. There are some large and very perfect hut circles on the N. slopes of the tor. As one approaches the tor, the Devonport leat is struck. The leat becomes a fine mountain torrent as it flows below Leather Tor, and rushes over the boulders with great tumult. Leather Tor Bridge spans the Meavy below Leather Tor Farm, and the view from the W. side is very picturesque. Above the bridge, on the E. bank of the stream, are the remains of an old blowing house.

From Leather Tor Farm take the road which leads up the hill ; it soon crosses the leat. Keep to the road till it turns sharply to the L. Here is Lowery Cross with its massive base. This lane will soon lead you to Nosworthy Bridge. Below the bridge the Meavy is joined by the Nillacombe, and it is rather a noisy meeting, especially after heavy rain. Further up the road towards Narrator the Dean comes down the valley and flows into the Meavy.

It is a land of streams just here. Very pleasant it is to listen to —   " The brooks;
    Muttering along the stones, a busy noise
    By day, a quiet sound in silent night."

The view from Nosworthy Bridge, looking up stream, is one of extreme beauty. With the brawling river in the foreground and the cone of Leather Tor soaring up in the background, it assumes the proportions of real grandeur, and is, I believe, the finest piece of real mountain scenery on the moor.

Among the trees on the R. are the ruins of Nosworthy Farm. On the E. bank of the river, about 100 yds. above the farm, where the path becomes narrow, you will come upon traces of the walls of an old shed. Here are nearly a dozen round hollows cut in the rocks, which were the old slag pounding hollows used by the tinners.

CHAPTER XII.

YELVERTON.

1—Meavy.   2—Bickleigh Vale.   3—Roborough Down.

Yelverton is built around a breezy common, and is in a
most healthy situation.   With such a fine expanse of
common, Yelverton folk can never complain of over-
crowding or of any lack of fresh air.   Of late years,
Yelverton has attracted an increasing number of visitors,
who come to enjoy the beautiful moors, for which it is a
good centre.

It stands on high ground, and has a much more genial
climate during the winter months than is experienced
further on Dartmoor.   In winter at Sheepstor the snow
sometimes covers the ground for days, when there is very
little to be seen at Dousland or Yelverton.   The place is
also blessed with a good deal of sunshine ; it has an
appreciably higher record than places further inland.

With the exception of the walks which I mention below,
all the beautiful walks accessible from Yelverton are fully
described in Chapters IX. and X. dealing with Sheepstor
and Dousland, so walk or train to Dousland and start
from there.

The other pleasant walks from Yelverton are as
follows : —

XII. 1.   **Meavy** ($1\frac{1}{2}$ m)   Turn down the lane which
runs parallel to the station road.   When you approach the
railway arch, turn sharply under the railway.   This lane
will bring you straight into Meavy, which I described in
my Dousland chapter.

XII. 2.   **Bickleigh Vale.**   Visitors to this neighbourhood
should walk through Bickleigh Vale, through which the
Plym flows.   Here are sylvan peeps of real beauty.
Alight at Plym Bridge Platform or Marsh Mills Station
and walk up the Vale to Bickleigh Station.

There is also a pleasant walk beside the Meavy from
Good-a-Meavy to Yelverton.

A visit may profitably be paid to Meavy.   The church
is in a very good condition of repair, and contains some

very early carving at the chancel arch, that may be pre-Norman, so rude is it.   Near the church is an old house of the Drake family, now a farm, and the village cross, and the famous Meavy oak, 27 ft. in circumference, with the trunk so decayed as to form an archway through which a person may walk erect.   It is supposed to have been standing here in the reign of King John.   The village chronicles relate that nine persons once dined within the hollow trunk, where a peat-stack may now be frequently seen, piled up as winter fuel.   Although the head of the tree be bald, the lower branches are still bright with foliage.

In the churchyard is an epitaph, a varient of others found elsewhere :—

> Our life is but a winter's day ;
> Some only breakfast, and then away :
> Others to dinner stay, and are full fed,
> The oldest man but sups and goes to bed.
> Large is his debt who lingers out the day ;
> Who goes the soonest has the least to pay.

The point here is that the stone commemorates the members of a family who died at the respective ages of 94, 88, 29 and 16.

XII, 3. **Roborough Down** is a fine tract of moor for a ramble. Roborough Rocks are passed on the right – a favourite picnic place for visitors. There are excellent golf links on Roborough Down at the Yelverton end.

CHAPTER XIII.

Some Dartmoor Worthies.

SIR JAMES BROOKE, **First Rajah of** Sarawak   A good
account of his life appears in " Beautiful Dartmoor," Part I.
which I will not repeat here; but I had some good notes

RAJAH BROOKE PARLEYING WITH THE NATIVE RAJAH
WHO PRECEDED HIM.

about him given me by Mr. Charles Calmady, of Horra-bridge, who, when he was a boy, knew him well.   He says :—" He was a man of a very distinguished appearance, about 5 ft. 10 ins. in height, with a slight but well proportioned figure.   His complexion was sallow, and his face rather heavily pitted with small pox.   One day we went to call at Burrator House, and he introduced us to Mr. and Mrs. Cruickshank who were staying with him. He placed his hand on my shoulder and pointing to Mrs. Cruickshank, said—' that lady standing there has the mark of a cut from a Chinese sword all down her back.' "

The circumstances were : —
One day the Sarawak Residency was suddenly surroun-ded by a band of Chinese Rebels, and being taken completely by surprise, the Rajah and his friends had to fly for their lives. Both the Cruickshanks were cut down and left for dead. The Rajah and a few followers succeeded in escaping by wading through what was thought to be an impassible swamp, and in an in-credibly short time he gathered an armed force, and before the rebels had time to make off with the loot, he surrounded the Residency and slaughter-ed every Chinaman he could find.   He was in time to save the Cruick-shanks, who, though left for dead were still alive.

Under medical care they both recovered and returned to England.

Mr. Calmady says he thinks he must be the only person alive to have attended the Rajah's funeral in 1868, but

Mr. Amos Shillibeer still living in Sheepstor was there.

RAJAH BROOKE

The Rajah's Tomb is in the N.E. corner of Sheepstor Churchyard under the shade of the great beech tree, and is made of red Aberdeen Granite.

He was a very remarkable man, and made Sarawak what it is, and his work has been so splendidly carried on by the second and third Rajah's.

FIRST RAJAH BROOK'S TOMB AT SHEEPSTOR.

THE SECOND RAJAH was buried by myself in August, 1921, two years after he died. The War Laws were still in force, tho' the war was actually over when he died, and the Government of the day would not allow his enbalmed body to be taken to Sarawak. The idea was to have an impressive funeral there to impress the Natives, but after two years it was felt certain the natives with their primitive minds would have forgotten he ever lived. So at last it was decided to bury him at Sheepstor. The present Rajah and Rajnee, and the widow were present at the funeral. The coffin which was made of very fine grained Sarawak wood, arrived the previous evening, and remained in the Church till the time of the funeral next day.

The grey granite forming the tomb was quarried in Sheep's Tor, and drawn down to the Churchyard by eleven horses, and through the Churchyard wall. It was cracked on the way down, so great a mass of granite is often liable to crack in this way.

HARRY TERRELL.

HARRY TERRELL

was a remarkable man in many ways. He was a simple child of nature and an accomplished horseman, a great hunter of fox and fulmart. He lived for many years at Burrator House, and finally sold it to the 1st Rajah Brooke. I could tell many tales of him, but lack of space prevents me giving more than one, in which he succeeded in deceiving that wily huntsman—the Rev. John Russell— Russell brought his hounds from North Devon for a week's hunting in the south.   Foxes were scarce in those days, and there was some fear that there might be a blank day.   Jack Russell was on such intimate terms with his hounds that the least variation in the behaviour of any one of them would attract his attention.

There is a peculiarity in the scent of a bagged fox ; if he has only been captured a short time he is not like a wild fox, and a great change has come over him which affects the scent he leaves behind him.

A confidential man with a bagged fox was instructed to lie down in the middle of a very thick brake.   When he heard Russell's horn, on leaving the meet, about $\frac{1}{4}$ mile off, he was to let go the fox and then lie quite still and quiet himself, until everyone was gone.

The hounds were thrown into one end of the brake and gradually drawn up to the fox, and a Billy Black was outside to view him away and distract attention by a superabundant amount of hallooing.   The hounds settled on their line and travelled right across Dartmoor and killed in the open. They eat their fox, and Russell never knew he had been cheated with a bagged fox, but always talked of it as a perfect run.   He was never told.

Terrell was born in Tavistock, on 12th April, in 1807, and died in London, March 18th, 1871.

JOHNNY ROBERTS was a mighty huntsman and an especially fine rider, and was huntsman of Mr. Pode's hounds, of Slade, Cornwood.

There is an absurd story of a great run, when Johnny Roberts rode his horse to a stand still, no one else up ; he took a promising looking horse out of a plough – no ploughman would think of refusing Johnny anything, and finished the run on him bareback, the only one at the death.   Johnny left behind him an immense reputation.

Some of the old hunting-men were perpetually referring to " Johnny Roberts' Day " with lamentations for a time of perfect, happy hunting, past and gone, never to be seen again.

A very large fox had been driven to earth and it was decided to take him out, which was a formidable undertaking.   Terrell's white rough terrier was " in " and they had to dig to her. As she never ceased fighting the fox, and "telling" about him, they could only dig to her "noising."

A dispute arose, and Terrell gave a very decided opinion, on which a well-known hunting man said :—

"Ah! it would not have been like that in Johnny Roberts' day. Terrell said, 'I was sartain Johnny Roberts would be drawed in my teeth. Johnny Roberts was a good sportsman, I've no doubt, but he had a forgitful lot of disciples.'"

They dug on and took out the fox, which had a huge mask and was very old.

RICHARD LAVERS OF TROWLESWORTHY.

RICHARD LAVERS. This fine old man lived at Trowlesworthy Warren for a great number of years. I knew him only in the later years of his life.

He was a wonderfully sturdy man, and a fine type of moorman. He took a keen interest in Freemasonry, and was possibly the oldest Mason in Devon.   He was a member of Lodge "Erme" 1091, Ivybridge, and for a very long period attended the Meetings.   He died on March 15th, 1915, and was buried on March 20th.

The morning brought a very deep drifting snow but the March sun melted 3 ft. in a day.   His coffin which was in a hearse was preceded by a long line of outriders on horseback, and the procession was a most dignified affair.

On that day Richard no doubt had his wish fulfilled. About two years before he died he paid a visit to the Vicar of Shaugh, and said he had one request he wanted the Vicar to grant.

"When I die, will you be sure and bury me beside my first wife."   The reply was—"Of course I will."

CHAPTER XIV.

Ancient Records of Dartmoor Parishes

PART 2.

CHURCHWARDENS' ACCOUNTS, 1567—1600.

These are contained in a book in a bad condition, and disreputable appearance.

The earliest book, which dates 1567 to 1602, has four separate Accounts each year and few are missing—First comes the Churchwardens' Accounts; then the Constables'—a very fine collection; then those of the Collectors for the Poor, and lastly the Surveyor's of the Wayes, the last named are in each case brief, but they contain an interesting account of the repairs of the highways and byways.

In dealing with a field so vast as the Parochial Records of nearly 400 years it is obviously only possible to give a few matters of interest.

The next book contains the Collectors' Accounts from 1611 to 1657. Then comes a serious gap to 1681, when the Churchwardens' and Constables' Accounts are renewed, but both are in the *same* account each year, from 1681 the Churchwardens' Accounts are continuous to the present day, and the Constables' Accounts 1681 to 1800.

Both are missing in the Civil Wars period. There are complete lists of Officers—The iiij men from 1565 to 1600 : the Churchwarden's 1554 to 1628 (and on to the present day in the Accounts) ; also a complete list of the Collectors of the Poor, 1568 to 1629; also of the Surveyors of the Wayes, 1569 to 1628.

The Altar.

Early in the reign of Elizabeth an order was made for the removal of the stone altars and Dean Prior obeyed the order, the stone was to be replaced by a table of wood.

1568.   For wryting the X Commandments —xxvs.
         Pd for makyn of the Communyon Tabell.—xd.
         Pd for iiij crooks of iron for the same tabell.—

E

The altar stone was sold in the following year.

1569.   Received for our Alter stone.—iijs. iiijd.
1576.   Payed for the Communyon Cuppe.—xxıjs. ijd.

This date agrees with the date inscribed on the cover of our Chalice, which was made at this time by Johns, a famous silversmith at Exeter in Elizabethan times.

At some time the bowl has been broken from the stem of the Cup.

1591.   Pd for mendying of the Communyon Cuppe.   ijd.
1573.   Pd for ij coverynges for the Communyon Tabell —iijs. iiijd.
1583.   Pd for wayssynge of the Church Ornementes for iij several tymes.—iijd.
1585.   Pd for a glassen bottell.—iijd.
1586.   Wasshyn of the communyon clothe. --
1595.   Pd for a forme in the Chancel. – xd.
1571.   Pd for a but (hassock) to lye before the Communyon tabell.—ijd.

The amount of wine used at Dean was always moderate.

1575.   Pd for wine for the Communyon.—ijd.
1581.   Pd for a bottell to keep wyne in.—6d.
1581.   Pd for a boxse to keep bryde in.—6d.
1581   Pd for the Syngen bred. - js.

This was the larger or priest's wafer; it is said to have been called the singing Bread because chants were sung while it was being made. This shows that the wafer was not forbidden at the Reformation, but it was still in use in 1581; support of this is seen in the smallness of the cover of our 1576 chalice. This small paten was made expressly for the use of the wafer.

At Tavistock 36 quarts were used at Easter. The quantity used in many parishes was a constant source of strife between the parish priest and the churchwardens. The quantity required at the Celebration of the Communion was used, and the bulk went into the priest's cellar; this is a liquid fact.

Recently, I was going through the Warden's Account of a Devon parish, date 1800. There was strife between the priest and churchwardens, and the priest claimed his wine on the ground of " Immemorial custom " and won his point. Henceforth, for many years, there was this charge—" *Pd to the minister in room of wine according to custom—£1 4s. od.*" A monstrous imposition.

The Font.

Dean Font is Norman, made of Devon red sandstone. It was painted once, why I cannot think, unless it was before the present lead lining was placed in it, and that the stone was porous.

1682. Pd for painting the King's Arms and setting up the sittenes in the Church and painting the pulpit and desk and vant.— £8 18s. 0d.

It was customary in preparing for Baptism, after the Cover had been unlocked and raised, to cover the font with a fair linen cloth. References to " *the font cloth* " are very rare in Wardens' Accounts. Dean has two such references.

1586. Wasshynge the vant cloth.—jd.
1597. Washynge the vant clothe.—jd.

During the Commonwealth the use of the font was forbidden and a pewter basin substituted. Dean still has its pewter basin.

Gifts.

Sometimes the Church Account was helped by gifts of money.

The Church made many gifts to Church building, &c.

1576. For the charge of the buldynge of the castell of Exon.—ijs.
1577. The Collections for the buldynge of the Church of Bath.—xijd.
1569. Pd to the relefe of them taken in Turkey.—xxd.
1577. Pd to iij other collectors of severall hospetalles.—xiijd.
1586. Pd towards the re-edifying of a Church in London.- xjd.

Visitations During This Period.

The Archdeacon's Visitation is Annual, and the Bishop's very frequent.

1567. Expenses at the Bishop's Vysytasion.
1567. Charge and Expense at the Archdecon's Vysytasion.—iijs.
1568. Pd for expenses at the Archdecon's Vysytasion.—ijs. ixd.
1574. Pd at the Bishop's Vysytacion.—iijs. ijd.
*1576. Pd at the bysshope (Archbishop) of Canterbury's Vysitation — vjs. iiijd.
Pd to the bysshope of Canterbury's Officers.—xijd.
1577. Pd at the bysshoppes vysytacion.—iiijs.
Pd more at Exon at the bysshoppe's curte (court)—iijs. iijd.
1583. Pd at the Archdeacon's Vysitatyon at Totnes and for our Articles and all other charges.—vs.
*1584 Pd at the Bysshop's Vysytacion of Canterye hodenn at Totynyes and for our expenses.—iiijs.
Pd at the Archdekens Vysytacion.

1595. Pd for our Artikelles at the Vysytacion.—js. iiijd.
       Pd for a collage in Kingston on Thems.—-xd.
1599. Pd for our Artikelles at the Visytayon.—js.

"*The Articles*" were "The Articles of Enquiry"
relating to the conduct of the Incumbent and the conduct
of the services during the past year, and other business.

* The Woodleigh Parish Books record these visitations
of the Archbishop, and a third in 1634 by Archbishop
Land.

The Office of Rural Dean was not instituted until 16—

The Bells.

In the Tudor Period, Dean Prior had four bells which
were old bells in 1567, when our Accounts begin; they
are recorded in the Certificate of the Parish goods issued
to the Church in 1553. (*See Part 2, Page 1.*)

These four bells were re-cast in 1734, evidently at the
expense of the Yarde family.

Here are some interesting stories :—

1568. Casting of the lytel bell, xijs. viijd. For setting up of the
       bell.—ijs. vjd.
       Pd to Robert Tolchard for mendyng and kepyng of the Bells.
       xiijd.
1569. Pd for makynge the jar (iron) work of the littell bell.—vjd.
1593. Pd John Tolchard for mendynge of the bell-frame and for
       grese,—xd.
       Pd for a bell coller and for a pott of oyle.—vjd.
1595. Pd to the Ringers on the Crownatyon (Coronation) Daye.
       —iijs. vjd.
       Pd for grese and oyle for the bells.—iiijd.
       Pd to Robert Tolchard for Kepynge of the Bells.—ijs. vjd.
1597. Pd to the Ringers the 17th day November.—xxd.
                       (Queen's Birthday.)

Books.

1568. Pd for a Communyon Booke.—viijd.
1570. Pd for an homelye booke.—xvjd.
1576. Pd for a newe homelye book.—xvjd.
1582. Pd for six littell books.—vjd.
1589. Pd for mendynge of the Church books, viz. : the bebell and
       the too communyon bookes.—iijs. iiijd,
1592. Pd for a new bending (binding) of the Communyon booke.—
       ijs. vjd.
1597. Pd for a bourck of prayers for her Majestye fflett.—iijs.

Robes.

1573. Pd for a Serpeles and a Rouchett (Rochet).—xviijs.

Church Repairs and Renewals.

1567. Pd for 2,000 lathe nayles.—iijs.
   ,, 1,500 shyndle pynnes.—iijs.
   ,, 1,000 shyndle stones (slates).—ijs.
1568. Pd for brode stones for the Church.—ijs. vjd.
   ,, fetching home the same.—vijd.
   ,, mendynge the Church geate.—ixd.
1569. Pd more for the iron work of the Church Geate.—vjd.
   Pd for lying and mendynge of the leddes.—xxxiijs. xd.
1574. Pd for tylinge in the Church.—ijd. (Two tiles only remain).
1576. Pd the glassyer for mendynge and glassynge our Church wyndows.—xxxs.
1584. Pd for mendynge of the stepel dore locke and the Church dore locke.
1588. Pd to the glassyer for putten newe glass and mendynge of our Church wyndows.—xvjs. viijd.
1590. Pd for a new cheste his locke, and kaye, and hemes (iron bands) – xiijs. vijd.
1592. Pd for glassynge of the Church windowes.—vjs. iiijd.
1593. Pd for a ladder for the puyche.
   ,, mendynge the sigge (seat) behend the Church dore.
     (This was there till the last restoration).
   Pd more for tomber for the same.—iiijs.
1594 Pd Would the plumbmer.—iljd.
   Pd to the plomber and carpenter for coming at severall tymes and expenses —ijs. xd.
   Pd for bryngynge some of the new ledde and for carydge back of the old ledde and expense.—xijs. vjd.
   Pd for expense when we weyhed the old ledde.– iiijd.
   Pd the carpenter for worke for the leddes.—xs. vjd.
   Pd for tymber and expenses.— xiijs.

(I). SOURCES OF THE INCOME FOR CHURCH EXPENSES.

THE CHURCH ALE was not, as is often assumed, a parish drunk, but a perfectly legitimate day's enjoyment. It was the parish feast, and drinking old English Ale played a part in it; some disgraced themselves as they do now, by taking too much.

These were the different ales held :—

The Ale was a periodical gathering of parishioners, which continued to be held into the eighteenth century. Its object was to raise funds through the medium of amusement. There were several kinds. I give the principal ones.

(1) **The Church Ale,** or Whitsun Ale, so called because from being generally held at Whitsuntide, was quite an important institution. The two churchwardens were the ale-givers, who, after collecting subscriptions in money and kind from the parishioners, gave a revel. This Ale was held in the Church House, wherein the churchwardens brewed and stored their ale and gave a feast, the proceeds of which were devoted to replenishing church funds and repairing the church.

(2) **The Clerk Ale,** was a feast held to increase the meagre salary of the parish clerk. It realized a fairly substantial sum—more than his salary would amount to in several years.

(3) **The Bid-Ale** was held when a parishioner had failed in his worldly calling, or to use a Dartmoor expression, *gone scat* ; or if he had met with an accident or some other misfortune depriving him of his livelihood. The Bid-Ale was not lacking in humour. With the proceeds of the feast which were handed over to him, the broken man was expected to make a feast of ale, and all that was left after the expenses of the feast were paid went to the unfortunate man to set him on his legs again for a renewed fight with the world.

(4) **Give-Ales,** were the legacies of individuals, and entirely gratuitous.

(5) **Bride-Ale,** was sold by a bride on her wedding day. She received whatever handsome price the guests choose to pay her for it.

(6) **Foot-Ale.** was the feast, in which liquor flowed freely, required from one entering on a new occupation.

(7) **Drink-lean,** was a contribution of tenants towards a potation or ale provided to entertain the lord or his steward.

There are still the remains of two Ale-Houses in this neighbourhood—one at Rattery, near the churchyard gate; the other at Widecombe, which is now the Parish Room.

Here I am dealing with The Church Ale, as a source of revenue for the Church Accounts and I give some instances at Dean.

1567. Received of the Church Ale.—xl. viijs. 0d.
1569.   ,,   ,,   ,,   iiijl. iijs. iiijd.

They realised different amounts in different years as not only the Churchwardens, but also the iiij men organised an Ale, and sometimes they were held more than once a year.

1576. The iiij men's Ale realised xl. viijs. ixd.
      The Wardens' Ale, iijl. viijs. 0d.

Compulsory Church Rates were unknown before Elizabeth's reign.

(2). THE HIRE OF CHURCH PROPERTY.

Another regular source of income was the hire of the Church Vessell and other parish property for the purpose of private brewings. There are hundreds of these records.

1568. Recd of Andrew Foxe for brewynge in the Church House.—xijd.
      Chrystopher Maddick for occupying the Chytell (the furnace) —vjd.
1580. Recd from Chrystopher Arscot for hire of ye vessell.—vjd. (the iron pot in which the ale was brewed).

The rent of these articles produced quite a regular income for the Church as they were hired so much each year.

Another source of income was profits from the Church Farm.

1568. Recd of Marjery Fell for a shepe.—iiijs. iiijd.

(3). GIFTS.

Sometimes the Church Account was helped by gifts of money :—

1578. Recd of the beneyvolence of the young men.—ijs. ijd.
1579. Margery Mudge's gift to the poure.—iijs. iiijd.

(4). SUNDRY SALES OF CHURCH PROPERTY.

1569. Old tymber.—iiijs. xd.
1573. Olde Iron.—iii'd.
1581. Recd for the Olde Bebell the sum of 3/-

(5). The Church Rate.

See the Rating List for the Collectors of the Poor for 1589, given in the plates in "Robert Furze, Gentleman."

(6). The Church Pytt.

For burial in the Church at a uniform charge of vjs. viijd. (See Church Pytt, p. 97).

DEAN AND THE POPE.

Peter's Pence or Romescot dates back to the Saxon period, and a tax of a penny on every hearth was sent to Rome. It was diverted to the Cathedrals by Henry VIII and ceased to be paid to Rome; restored by Mary, and again changed by Elizabeth.

It is called Peter's Farthings at Milton Abbot in 1588.

These were made at Dean long after they ceased in most parishes.

1582.   Pd for Peter's Pynce.—vid

It should be noted that vid. did not represent the amount paid to Peter. A certain amount was fixed for the parish to pay, and the amount raised always fell short of the assessment and the deficit was made up from the Churchwarden's Accounts. This vid. represents this deficit.

The monks of Buckfast recently made this amusing retort in "Chimes" :—

> "We learn from *The Tablet* that our neighbour, the Anglican Vicar of Dean Prior, has just discovered in the churchwarden's accounts entries shewing the payment of Peter's Pence in that parish as late as 1597. It is to be doubted whether the Pence, paid nearly 40 years after the accession of Elizabeth, ever found their way to Peter! Possibly not."

There are frequent payments to Pardoners. A Pardoner was one who went about with the Pope's Indulgences in his pocket to sell to the highest bidder. The amounts of the payments differ at Dean.

1575.   Pd to a Pardner—occurs this year no less than four times.

Several generations later Dean evidently needed pardon.

1700.   Pd for a Proclamation against immorality and prophaness. 1s. 0d.

LIST OF THESE PAYMENTS.

1569.   Pd for Peter's Rent.—vjd.
1570.   ,,   Pardon.—vjd.
1571.   ,,   ,,   vjd.
1575.   Pd to a Pardener.—vjd. (4 men's Ale)
              ,,   Pardner   iiijd.
              ,,   Pardner   vjd.
              ,,   Pardner   vjd.
1580.   Pd to a pure (poor) pardoner.—iiijd.
1582.   Pd for Peter's Pynce.—vjd.
1584.   At the Archedetions Vysytation at Tottnys Pd for our
        expenses and for Peter's Pardoner.—
1586,   Pd for Peter's Pens.—vjd.
1592,   Pd the Pardner. vjd.
1594.   Pd to ix, Pardners at severall tyemes.—ijs, iiijd.
        Pd to ij pardners more —vjd.
1594.   Pd for the lyenge in of our byll for the *recusant.*—xijd.
1595.   Pd for Peter's Penes.—vjd.
1596.   Pd for the lyeing in our bill and Peters Pens.—xd.
        Pd for a Pardoner that Voyse deleverd.—vjd.
1597.   ,,   Peters Penys and for lyeing in of our bill.—xd.
1594.   ,,   bringing in of our bill and Peters Pence.—js. od.

The Church Pytt.

This refers to the custom of burials under the Church floor.

This revolting and loathesome method of burial was
much in use through Elizabeth's reign.

In consequence of these burials the Churches became
regular pest houses, and were often the cause of the grave
outbreaks of plague so common in those days.

For burials in the Church the charge over all England
seems to have been the same,—vis. viijd.

Under the floor was called the Church Pytt.

There are many such records in Dean.

1568.   Recd for Symon Mardale'c buriall in the Church Pytt.—
        vjs. viijd.
1574.   Recd for Walter Tolchard's grave in the Pytt—vjs. viijd.
1568.   Johan Shere for her husband's buryal in the Church Pytt.—
        vjs. viijd
1569.   S. Foxe   ditto
1581.   Pd to John Dunridge for Christopher Voyse's ditto-vjs. viijd.
1578.   Rd of Robert Furze for a grave for his sonne in the Church—
        vjs. viijd.
1581.   Rd of Margerye Stidston for her father's grave in the
        Church.—vjs. viijd.

There is this curious record :

1597.　Pd to . . . for makynge plene fo the walkes and the pet in the Church.—xd.

The Church floor was of earth ; this man levelled and made plain the paths, and also shewed where the burials were taking place then.

Outside the Church Porch on the west side, there is still an ossuary to which the bones were removed when the Church pytt became overcrowded. On Sundays Dean people sit in Church with their feet resting on the bones of their ancestors.

These Dean records show that there was uniformity to the Charges for ' buryall in ye Church Pytt,' the popular view was otherwise.

This is illustrated at Hartland, where there used to be this verse on a tomb some years ago :—

> " Here lies I at the Church Door ;
> Here lies I because I'se poor,
> The further in, the more they pay
> But here lies I as warm as they."

A distinction of this kind is hateful, but it is not confined to Christian times. A few years before I went to Alfriston, excavations for the foundations of a new house, revealed the site of an ancient Pagan burial ground, said to have been Saxon—the field was named " Sanctuary." The richer folk had been buried with their treasures in careful order, the poor had been thrown into a pit anyhow.

About 100 burials were located, and this feature was noticeable. Most of the finds are exhibited in the Lewes Museum now.

The Churchyard.

1568.　Pd for mendynge of the Church Geate.—ixd.
1574.　Pd for a rope for the Church Geate.—iijs
1572.　Pd for makynge of the Church Yarthe Hagges. – ijs. ijd.
1586.　Pd for makynge of the Church Yard hagge beside the wode.

(Before the road was widened there was a belt of trees at the west-end).

1586.   Pd to Robt. Tolchard for mendynge the Churchyard geate.
   xiijd.
   Pd more for a springe for the Churchyard geate.—iiijd.
1580.   Pd for mendynge of the polye (pulley) of the Church geate.

(This primitive form of opening and shutting a gate is still in use at Sheepstor. The rope often rots and has to be renewed, but the polye (pulley) lasts years.)

THE SORROWS OF DEAN.

At Dean in 1590, *the plague carried off at least* 50 *people.* There were 56 burials that year, 51 of which took place in the four months, July to October. This against the annual average of about 6 each year. One family was wiped out. There are these notes in the Register,--" Here the Plague began, ... here the Plague ended."

In 1678 there were 22 burials but there is no record of the nature of the outbreak.

In 1866 there was a grave outbreak of smallpox, in which the Vicar of Dean died of smallpox.

Curiosities.

Cappes.
   Among many very curious records is this :—

1576,   Pd for the discharge of the parish for not wearing of
   Cappes.—vs.

To help the Cap Trade in 1570 a Statute was passed which ordered every male person over six years old to wear a woollen cappe, on sondaies & holy daies. The penalty for each transgression was 3/4. Dean was fined 5/- for its transgression.

The Parish Herse.

Another curious record which occurs several times :—

1575.   For nelles to mend the herse with.—ijd.
1714.   Pd for a black herse cloth.—£1 12s. 6d.
1770.   Pd for cleaning the black clothe. - 1s. 0d.

The herse was not a funeral car, but a frame which was placed over the shrouded body when it was brough to the church for burial, before coffins were in common use. The herse was removed when the body was brought to the grave.

About 1720 Coffins began to be used, but they were expensive.

1723.   Pd for a coffin.—9/-
1729.   John Ellel for a coffin for him.—9/-
1569.   Received towards the makynge ofthe Jurerolose.—iijs iiijd.
1576.   Paid for a Creste. *i.e.* A ridge tile. The ridge tile on a
          gable was often surmounted with a family crest, hence
          the word is applied to the tile itself.
1569.   Pd for bredd and drynke when the tree fylled down in the
          Wylljke (village)—iiijd.

Evidently it had to be removed from the road.

Dean and Marley had many experiences of this in the terrible gales of the autumn of 1929.

Some Ancient Records of Sheepstor.

The vicarage of Sheepstor had not always a resident incumbent, a Mr. Smith was vicar of Sheepstor as well as Bickleigh, and divine service was held in Sheepstor only once in three weeks. In the book of Parish Expenses we find, 1809, for eight bottles of wine, £1 13s. 5d., 1812, for five bottles for the sacrament, and five for the minister £2 8s. od. After this the entry is not specified for wine, but as Mr. Smith's bill, £2 os. od., or £2 1s. 3d.: in 1824 his bill amounted up to £3 15s. 6d.

The tradition is that there was a stone seat about the space where is now the village cross, and that after service Mr. Smith came there and, sitting with the village elders, produced and drank the contents of these bottles. The story as now told is that they tippled whiskey, but it would appear from the entries in the parish book that it was wine they drank, and indeed at the time whiskey was hardly drank in England. The Holy Communion was celebrated four times in the year, but after a while was reduced to three times, and in 1835 only once.

The Sheepstor people insist on it that it was here that the incident occurred (which has been told of other churches with a non-resident vicar, and only occasional services) that the vicar was prevented from entering the pulpit by his clerk, being told that " th' ould guse had bin a' settin' a brude there all the week, and 'twere a cruel shame to disturb her."

Some of the entries in the Parish Account Book are amusing – the spelling is extraordinary –1728, for the Dane Ruler, expenses 4d., 1733, spent when Dan ruler came to voisitt, 1/-, 1742, for a bottle of wine when the Dean Ruler came to visit, 3/-; and this seems to have been what henceforth the Rural Dean expected.

There are repeated entries of payments for the killing of foxes, badgers, otters.

1719, for killing a young fixen and a young fox,				6s.	8d.
1723, ,,	,,	8 fitches and a hedgehog,	-	1s.	3d.
1750, ,,	,,	an orter,	-	2s.	6d.
1762, ,,	,,	4 foxes,	£1	os.	od.
		4 oater and 1 bager	-	3s.	od.

There was money given to wandering visitors in distress, but never largely.

1729, given to 2 sealors that logs (lost) teir (their) ship,	-	-	2s. od.
1732, Too 2 sealors that mad thear escape from Turkey with 28 men,	-	-	2s. 6d.
1738, to a man that has his tounge cut out of his mouth,	-	-	2s. od.

We have had some specimens of Sheepstor spelling, here are some more :—

1734, pd. for carigg of Lien	-	-	3s. 2d.
1735, pd. for a skittile tnat the prish was oner			2s. od.

The book containing distressments for the poor contains as well some curious matter. At one time the great drag on the parish funds was one Cherry, for whose breast the parish provided figs periodically.

CHAPTER XV.

The Poet's Corner.

THAT the wrestling was attended with danger to life
or limb cannot be doubted.   At Mary Tavy, in the
churchyard, is the tombstone of John Hawkins,
blacksmith, 1721 :—

> Here buried were some years before,
> His two wives and five children more :
> One Thomas named, whose fate was such
> To lose his life by wrestling much.
> Which may a warning be to all
> How they into such pastimes fall.

LITTLE JAN.

There is a Cornish ballad of a wrestling match between
Will Trefry and " Little Jan ":—

> I sing of champions bold
> That wrestled, not for gold,
>   And all the cry was Will Trefry !
> That he should win the day.
> So Will Trefry, Huzzah !
> The ladies clap their hands and cry
>   Trefry ! Trefry ! Huzzah
>
> Then up sprang Little Jan,
> A lad scarce grown a man,
>   He said, Trefry ! I wot I'll try
> A hitch with thee this day.
> So little Jan, Huzzah !
> The ladies clap their hands and cry
>   O little Jan, Huzzah !
>
> They wrestled on the ground,
> His match Trefry had found,
>   And back he bore, in struggle sore,
> He felt his force give way ;
> So little Jan ! Huzzah !
> So some did say – but others nay.
>   Trefry, Trefry ! Huzzah !
>
> Then with a desperate toss
> Will showed the flying hoss.
>   And little Jan fell on the tan,
> And never more he spoke.
> O little Jan ! alack !
> The ladies say ; O woe's the day,
>   O little Jan—alack !

The Elfords had a mansion at Yelverton, which is actually Elford's Town. The earliest Elford of whom anything is known was John Elford who lived during the fifteenth century and whose son, also John, was buried at Sheepstor in 1517. They were a sporting family, and a ballad has been preserved relative to a doe from their park :

THE SILLY DOE.

Give ear unto my mournful song,
  Gay huntsmen every one,
And unto you I will relate
  My sad and doleful moan.
O here I be a silly Doe,
  From Elford Park I strayed,
In leaving of my company
  Myself to death betrayed.

The master said I must be slain
  For 'scaping from his bounds :
" O keeper, wind the hunting horn,
  And chase him with your hounds."
A Duke of royal blood was there,
  And hounds of noble race ;
They gathered in a rout next day,
  And after me gave chase.

They roused me up one winter morn,
  The frost it cut my feet,
My red, red blood came trickling down,
  And made the scent lie sweet.
For many a mile they did me run,
  Before the sun went down,
Then I was brought to give a fun,
  And fall upon the groun'.

The first rode up, it was the Duke ;
  Said he, " I'll have my will ! "
A blade from out his belt he drew
  My sweet red blood to spill.
So with good cheer they murdered me,
  As I lay on the ground ;
My harmless life it bled away,
  Brave huntsmen cheering round.*

*The ballad with its delightful air is given in the Garland of Country
  Song. Methuen & Co, London.

SHAVERCOMBE.

Where the Shavercombe wends
    A way to the Plym,
And never ends
    Its murmured hymn,
Is a dainty glen,
    Like a gem encased
By the dreary fen
    And the moorland waste.

Atop of the dell
    A waterfall
Like a silver bell
    To the moor doth call,
And drops sweet foam
    On a pool, steel-blue
        Where the ripples roam,
    Smiling at you.

Where the mountain ash
    Is the only tree
Bright with the splash
    Of the Shavercombe's glee;
And the milkwort mild
    Is the only flower
        And the only child
        Of this secret bower.   G.M.P.

One notion anciently held on the moor, was that the souls of unbaptised babes that had died passed wailing in the wind.

The wind blows cold on waste and wold,
    It bloweth night and day ;
The souls go by 'twixt earth and sky,
    Impatient, cannot stay.
They fly in clouds and flap their shrouds,
    When full the moon doth sail,
In dead of night, when lacketh light,
    We hear them pipe and wail.

And many a soul with des'late howl,
    Doth rattle at the door,
Or rove and rout, with dance and shout,
    Around the granite tor.
We hear a soul 'i th' chimney growl,
    That's drenched with the rain,
To wring the wet from winding sheet,
    And see the fire 'l were fain.

Bullaven Farm Hotel,

Harford, near Ivybridge, S. Devon.

TELEPHONE IVYBRIDGE 40Y2.

Situated actually on the moor, but with every comfort.

ELECTRIC LIGHT.   CENTRAL HEATING.

SEPARATE TABLES.   30 BEDROOMS.

TENNIS COURTS.

PRIVATE 9 HOLE GOLF COURSE.

:   :   SWIMMING POOL.   :   :

HUNTERS, HACKS and CHILDREN'S PONIES.

(instruction given).

Inclusive Terms from 3½ Guineas.

APPLY SECRETARY.

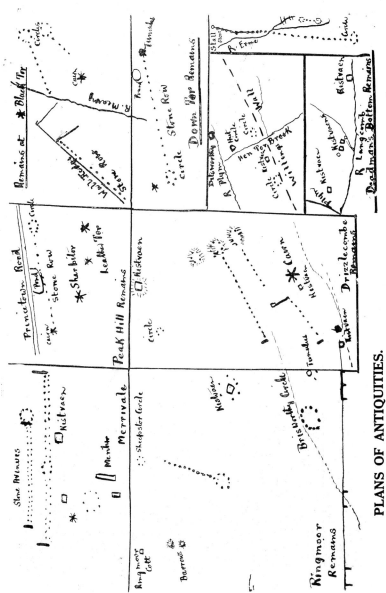

PLANS OF ANTIQUITIES.

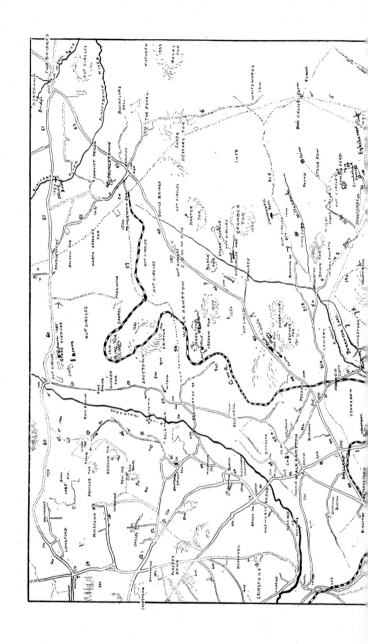

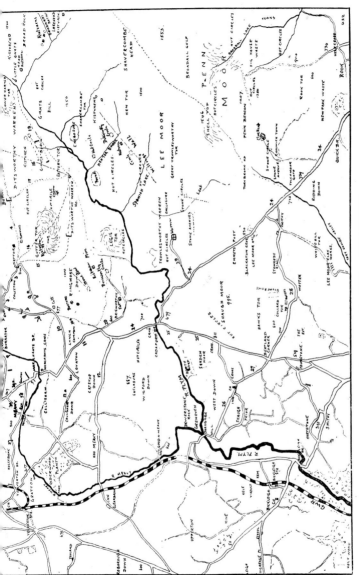

MAP OF THE S.W. QUARTER.

NOTES.

NOTES.

NOTES.